GW01158497

MASTERING SOLDIERS

New Directions in Anthropology
General Editor: **Jacqueline Waldren**, *Institute of Social Anthropology, University of Oxford*

MASTERING SOLDIERS

Conflict, Emotions, and the Enemy
in an Israeli Military Unit

Eyal Ben-Ari

Berghahn Books
New York • Oxford

First published in 1998 by
Berghahn Books

Library of Congress Cataloging-in-Publication Data
Ben-Ari, Eyal, 1953–
  Mastering soldiers : conflict, emotions, and the enemy in an Israeli
military unit / Eyal Ben-Ari.
      p.   cm. -- (New directions in anthropology : v. 10)
  Includes bibliographical references (p.   ) and index.
  ISBN 1-57181-145-1 (alk. paper).
    1. Sociology, Military--Israel. 2. Israel--Armed Forces--Reserves.
  3. Israel--Armed Forces--Military life. 4. Experiential learning--Israel.
  I. Title. II. Series.
U21.5.B46 1998
306.2'7'.095694--dc21   97-42089
                                                CIP

British Library Cataloguing in Publication Data
A catalogue record for this book is available from
the British Library.

Printed in the United States on acid-free paper

For Shlomo and Margalit

CONTENTS

PREFACE

> Interpretive ethnography is... a descriptive enterprise, which promises neither to uncover "how it feels" to get inside a native's skin nor to facilitate causal generalization, but rather through its organization to promote at once a taste for detail and a sense of pattern and to articulate something about the ways that cultures work by showing what they "mean" – Rosaldo, *Knowledge and Passion*

*T*his book is an interpretive ethnography of a battalion of Israeli infantry reserves. Ethnographies, the standard fare of anthropological work, are detailed studies of the lives and activities of groups of people. These ethnographic studies depend to a great degree on firsthand observations of the way people act, believe, and feel in concrete situations. Along these lines, this volume is devoted to uncovering the meanings of military service for the soldiers of this unit. It is based on eight years of participant-observation during which I served as an officer in the battalion.

Almost any topic that anthropology deals with is subject to a host of connotations, viewpoints, and pre-conceptions. The topic of the Israeli military, however, is one where these understandings may be particularly strong. The Israeli Defence Forces (IDF) are viewed through a variety of prisms: the prism of the Israeli-Arab conflicts (of which the Israeli-Palestinian conflict is only one); the prism of popular glorification and moral denigration attendant on the Israeli military following the war in Lebanon and the Intifada (the Palestinian Uprising); the prism of the American military in the wake of the Vietnam debacle as somehow

morally tainted and therefore not 'worthy' of anthropological research
(see Simons 1997); and, no less importantly, the prism of what Michael
Mann (1987) has termed "mass-spectator militarism" – a fascination
with 'things military' as depicted in the electronic media (the coalition
forces in the Gulf War, for example).

Against this politically fraught background, I think it worthwhile to
place my study in its personal and historical context. I do so in order to
clarify how my social position has facilitated (and limited) certain
insights into Israeli military life. Essentially, my experience can be
characterized as a movement from induction *into* military life to inquiry
about military life.

Like most (Jewish) Israeli boys aged 18, I began my term of national
service at the beginning of 1972. With the naive view that distinguished
many young men at that period, I considered myself doubly
unfortunate. On the one hand, poor eyesight precluded my joining one
of the IDF's combat units. On the other hand, I thought I had "missed
out" on the glories and the attendant prestige of the 1967 Six-Day War.
Nevertheless, I resolved to do my best and, after basic training, went to
a variety of courses on army personnel administration (receiving merits
of excellence). In June 1973 I entered officers' training (in Israel there are
no academies, and officers come out of the enlisted ranks). I was still a
nineteen-year-old officers' cadet when the Yom Kippur War of 1973
broke out.

Being cadets, we were deemed by the army to be of equivalent
combat quality to infantry soldiers and thus on the first day of the war
we were sent to the Sinai. The seeds of this book were sown between the
6th of October and the 24th of that month when I was shot by an
Egyptian sniper in the city of Suez. It was during that war that I began
(at that time only vaguely) to be aware of Israel's vulnerability and of my
own naivete. Mine was what the Americans in the Second World War
referred to as a "Hollywood wound" (Fussell 1989:254) – one just severe
enough to require treatment at home, but without the need for
amputation or threat of permanent disfigurement. Consequently, after a
few weeks I ran away from a military convalescent installation to rejoin
the officers' course, which I was afraid of missing.

Upon finishing officers' training I became an adjutant, an
administrative officer or military bureaucrat in charge of personnel
matters. Subsequently, I have served in such a noncombatant support
role in front-line combat units for the rest of my army career. I first
served in a unit of regular paratroopers, and then, when I entered the

reserves, with another paratrooper unit. During Israel's debacle in Lebanon, I was fortunate to be away doing anthropological fieldwork in Japan and writing my Ph.D thesis in England. Upon my return to Israel, I again volunteered to be in a front-line unit and was with my new unit – a battalion of infantry reserves about which I have written this book – for eight years between 1985 and 1992.

The real beginnings of this volume lie in my experience of the Intifada (the Palestinian Uprising). My unit was deployed in the Hebron area (a city to the south of Jerusalem). The battalion performed all of the "usual" activities IDF units were (and still are) entrusted with in the occupied territories: setting up roadblocks, maintaining patrols, and carrying out arrests. During and especially after this period I found myself asking questions and seeking understandings in ways I had never done before. The curious combination of troubled citizen and anthropologist which has accompanied me ever since returning from my studies outside of Israel led me to ask: how do army reservists interrelate and reconcile their experiences of serving in the territories during the Intifada with those of living their "normal" everyday Israeli lives?

I attempted to answer these questions by writing a piece based on my impressions and observations as a deeply troubled participant. The piece was published outside of Israel in the journal *Cultural Anthropology* (Ben-Ari 1989), and in Israel (in Hebrew) in a book devoted to studying the impact of the Intifada on Israeli society (Gal 1990). During that period I did not carry out systematic field research, nor did I envisage a more comprehensive project. But as I wrote the piece I began to be preoccupied (and often troubled) by wider, perhaps deeper, issues. I began to feel that these issues were related not only to the Palestinian Uprising but to Israeli army service in general - to such questions as what soldiering means for reservists? what motivates reservists? What problems are associated with the transition between civilian and army lives? And, how is military identity related to citizenship and masculinity?

I felt that in order to get at these issues I needed to undertake a more systematic study of the unit, and then to write an ethnography about it. Being an anthropologist I decided to apply my professional expertise to my personal experience as a reservist. In other words, I decided to utilize my professional anthropological capabilities (honed outside of Israel on Japanese material) to write a broader, more wide ranging ethnography of my battalion. This book is the product of that effort.

All translations are mine unless otherwise noted.

ACKNOWLEDGEMENTS

I would like to thank Sarit Ben-Yakar for research assistance as well as for offering a variety of insightful comments and suggestions. Helpful criticisms on earlier versions of the text were offered by Edna Ben-Ari, Efrat Ben-Ze'ev, Marion Berghahn, Brian Farrel, Harvey Goldberg, Sarit Helman, Danny Kaplan, Tamar Katriel, Rotem Kowner, David Kuhn, Edna Levy-Schreiber, Tamar Liebes, Pamela Lubell, Baruch Nevo, Ofra Nevo, Susan Sered, Martin van Creveld, Jacqueline Waldren, and Judith Wrubel. In addition, this book has greatly benefitted from fruitful continuing discussions with Edna Lomsky-Feder. I would also like to thank participants at the following seminars where I presented talks related to this volume: the Departments of Anthropology at The University of Wisconsin (Madison), Yale University, and The University of Michigan, and the Departments of Sociology at Jagellonian University (Cracow), The National University of Singapore, and The University of Hong Kong.

Financial support for different stages of the project was provided by The Shaine Center of the Department of Sociology and Anthropology of the Hebrew University, The Harry S. Truman Research Institute of the Hebrew University, and The U.S. Army Research Institute through its European Coordination Office.

The volume was written in three places: the comfortable surroundings of the Department of Anthropology at the University of Wisconsin, Madison, the supportive environment of the Department of Japanese Studies at the National University of Singapore, and the rather harried circumstances of (my home) the Department of Sociology and Anthropology of the Hebrew University of Jerusalem. I would like to thank the staff of all of these departments for constant help and support.

A group of soldiers preparing for live-fire battalion exercise. Equipment is checked and final orders given. Israel's southern desert, 1991.

The outgoing and incoming battalion commanders during a briefing relating to deployment in the occupied territories. Hebron, 1989.

Above and below: End of 10 days of training: a return to civilian life. Last day of duty, a camp in Israel's southern desert, 1989.

Briefing for commanders. A live-fire battalion exercise, Israel's southern desert, 1989.

Patrolling Hebron, 1989

Commander's briefing. Hebron, 1989.

Myself in the officers' sleeping quarters drinking Diet Coke. Hebron, 1990.

Introduction

*M*ost soldiers know what "soldiering" and "commanding" entail. They can, for example, easily furnish illustrations of competence or incompetence in training or combat, evaluate concrete instances of professional conduct, prescribe appropriate behaviors, as well as discuss and analyze proper ways of producing "good soldiers." But what is the nature of this kind of military knowledge? How is it organized? In what way is it applied? Where is it "located"? This book represents an attempt to answer these questions. It does so by examining the main assumptions about, and images of, "conflict," "soldiering," the "use of military force," and the "enemy" that are held by soldiers and officers in a select unit of the Israel Defence Forces (IDF). To use a pair of rather old fashioned words, this volume represents a study of the "world view of soldiership."

Given the centrality of the armed forces in most, if not all, contemporary societies it is not surprising that military knowledge is both substantial and extensive. But this general category of "military knowledge" actually encompasses different kinds of expertise and different types of "know-how." Let me give a number of examples in order to delineate the sort of ongoing knowledge of "soldiering" that I refer to. Military doctrines (themselves part of wider security doctrines) form a central part of the social knowledge of military matters. These sets of authoritative principles – formulated by generals, politicians and related experts – guide the design of force structure and the conduct of operations (Levite 1989). While field officers and soldiers often have a good idea of how these precepts are exemplified or actualized in the ebb and flow of their everyday lives, military doctrines form a rather general background for routine soldiering. Another kind of knowledge of military matters is represented in the expert investigations of social scientists who study such things as military leadership, motivation or cohesion. These experts attempt to produce systematic theories and postulates that help improve military performance (see Gabriel 1987). Although some of this thinking seeps into the reasoning of soldiers and officers in field units, it does so in a peculiarly partial way. While military men may use social scientific concepts – borrowed from psychology or management studies, for example – they tend to use only some ideas or purported causal relations between variables with little or no systematic or coherent testing of their "pet" theories.

Some of the knowledge I refer to – the everyday, common-sense, normal understandings of "soldiering" and "commanding" – is found in the handbooks, primers, or guides that are regularly published by military organizations. But these books, for all their "how-to" orientation, are basically sets of rules and prescriptions. Though contributing to the performance of tasks, they can never cover all the exigencies of military activities let alone apply to the dynamic and changing environment within which military people operate. Other areas of this kind of knowledge appear in the volumes devoted to military history or biography. The knowledge conveyed in these books is part of the worldly wisdom officers and soldiers apply to the routines and extraordinary events of military life. Accordingly, the kind of knowledge I focus on is primarily practical and experiential, or what Donald Schon (1987) has termed knowledge-in-action. The practical and experiential nature of this military expertise implies, for instance, that while military people do not (and may not be able to) fully define such terms as "discipline," "leadership," or "performance," they rely on experience to assess the practical meaning of these terms as they are applied to individual soldiers, officers or even whole units (see also Walker 1992:309). The questions thus still remain: What is the nature of this kind of everyday military knowledge? How is this knowledge – part learned, part past experience, and part worldly wisdom – organized so that soldiers and officers can (with little reflection) carry out a host of what social scientists call cognitive tasks: describe, evaluate, characterize, diagnose, advise or prescribe?

I address these questions through a focus on the models – later I term them "folk" models or "lay" theories[1] – that members of the armed forces have of military service and of "soldiering" and "commanding." In other words, my aim is to uncover the assumptions, images, and interpretive schemes that lie at base of mundane or common sense military knowledge. By such terms as "mundane" or "common sense" I do not mean that this knowledge is simplistic, nor do I imply that it is unimportant. Rather, these terms refer to the unquestioned knowledge that "everyone knows"; to what Geertz (1983) has termed the "of-courseness" of common sense understandings. These models are of great importance because they are the basic points of reference for "what we are" and "what we are trying to do" through which military reality is constructed.

This book proceeds from the assumption that conceptions of combat, performance, or antagonists form the basis for interpreting the environment within which armies operate. It examines a case study of a battalion of elite[2] infantry reserves of the Israel Defence Forces (IDF). Based on a number of years of participant-observation, this analysis is basically ethnographic in its approach. In order to situate my study in relation to contemporary scholarship about the military and about the IDF, and in order to clearly identify the issues I have singled out for analysis, let me answer three questions in the framework of this introduction: Why focus on the "folk" models of soldiers? Why the Israeli military? And why the specific case I have chosen to study?

From Military Traditions to Military Culture

Writing in the mid-1970s, Luttwak and Horowitz (1975) contended that the IDF neither had its own military traditions nor imported other countries' traditions as virtually all postcolonial armies had done. Rather, the growth of the Israeli army has been marked, according to them, by a turmoil of innovation, controversy, and debate. Luttwak and Horowitz were right in noting that the Israeli army (especially in the first decade of its existence) had no "tradition" as the term is used in the British, American, or French forces. At the same time however, the IDF was based from its beginnings on certain principles borrowed both from the British military and from pre-state army organizations like the Haganah and the Palmach (Sheffy 1991; Ben-Eliezer 1995a, 1995b).[3]

In the past decade or so, however, a number of studies have shown how the Israeli military is characterized by some rather concrete organizational ideologies and tenets. Hasdai (1982) showed how two typical modes of thinking found in the Israeli army were related to decision making and promotion. Horowitz (1982) later wrote of the doctrines and tacit doctrines that permeate the Israeli military world view, while other scholars such as Kellet (1982:250) have observed the importance of understanding the basic assumptions about mutual responsibility and support which lie behind the Israeli army's tactical doctrines. In a similar vein, Sheffy (1991) has meticulously traced the origins of the fighting doctrine of the IDF back to the officers' courses of the pre-state Haganah.

Studies carried out outside of Israel echo a growing concern with understanding the way the managerial and organizational ideologies of the military constrain or facilitate the operation of forces (Feld 1977; Buck and Korb 1981; Dunivin 1994). While emphasizing the need to comprehend the interpretive side of military life, these kinds of works (carried out within Israel and outside of it) often still revolve around the "traditionality" – i.e. the authoritative conventions, practices, and ways of thinking – of the armed forces.

It is against this background that my study suggests a subtle shift of focus from military "traditions" to the culture of military organizations. The advantages of such a shift rest in widening the subjects of military related research into two hitherto little explored areas. In this way we may be able to focus less on the existence (or absence) of some military legacy but more on the ways in which military meanings are organized and used. Such a shift also may allow us to concentrate less on the way generals understand military matters than on how soldiers and officers in field units make sense of soldiering and commanding.

My suggestion about examining the "folk" models of military people should be seen in this light. It is around such models (or lay theories) that military cultures are internally organized. To reiterate, because these models are the basic points of reference for "what we are" and "what we are trying to do" through which people's reality is constructed, they establish points of reference that allow action to be interpreted, evaluated and prescribed.

Why the Israeli Military?

The Israeli army, in Reuven Gal's words, was founded in the crucible of war, born in the battlefield (1986:29), it is a fighting army. On the one hand, this image has fired literary and popular imaginations and led them to portray Israel romantically as a nation of soldiers disciplined to the rigors of frequent and long years of service. On the other hand, this representation has colored scholarly depictions of the "typical" soldier. This "exemplary" figure has frequently been portrayed as a professional whose experience in the military has been characterized by high motivation, considerable technical skills, a general acceptance of Zionist ideology, and an ethos of mutual responsibility on and off the battlefield.

A number of reasons underlie the scholarly interest in, and preoccupation with, these highly capable soldiers. First, the abundance of combat situations in which excellence is said to have figured as the primary element deciding victory or defeat has accentuated the role of these soldiers. Second, an emphasis on their excellence and professionalism has long served the interests of Israel's military authorities in setting up examples for recruits and in justifying the kinds of rewards the army offers its troops. Third, the expertise and relative success of the IDF has perforce drawn the attention of students of other armies to its elite forces as a model to emulate (see Van Creveld 1977:120). In this sense, Israel's select forces constitute an ideal "laboratory" for analyzing the issues I have singled out for study. Along these lines, if we aim at uncovering the everyday, common sense understandings of "soldiering" and "commanding," then combat units would seem the logical place to begin our inquiry[4].

Yet a certain kind of combat unit seems to be especially important for research in this respect. Despite the advent of various technological innovations in the military – as evinced in the Gulf (or what is sometimes known as the Microwave) War – it remains true militarily that only ground troops can take and hold land. In this respect, however, the infantry, in contrast to the artillery or the armored corps, includes those soldiers who have the most intense "hands on" relationship with the enemy. It is these "foot" soldiers who must grapple most powerfully with the stresses of combat and the perils of killing (Rieber and Kelly 1991: 17; Grossman 1995). This point can be put picturesquely following Grossman (1995: 108) and Dyer (1985): if gunners fire at grid references they cannot see, submarine crews fire torpedoes at ships (and not at the men in them); and if tank crews fire at tanks, infantry soldiers face the direct task of firing at other human beings. Thus I suggest that it is worthwhile to study units of the infantry, *the* military arm in which the prototypical pattern of face-to-face combat against antagonists takes place.

In effect, however, a good part of the IDF's "choice" soldiers are reservists – soldiers who are either mobilized yearly for routine tasks or activated in times of crisis. As a host of scholars have noted, although there are hints of transformation in the IDF, reservists still comprise the bulk and most important part of Israel's forces (Levite 1989: 34; Cohen 1995). The United States Army has only recently moved towards implementing the concept of "total force" in which reserve units are held to training standards and assigned combat missions equivalent to those of the permanent troops (Moskos 1988:47). In contrast to the American, British, and German settings, there seems to be less criticism from Israeli regulars about the abilities of reservists to perform on the battlefield (Walker 1992: 303). In Israel, the concept of "total force," or its equivalent has been the norm rather than the exception. Moreover, because of the internal organization of the IDF, all reservists initially serve in the standing army, and reserve troops are socialized by (and in many ways are also active socializers of) members of the permanent forces.[5] Thus for research purposes we can safely assume many basic commonalities of orientations and knowledge between elite elements whether they be regular or reserve units.

Why This Case?

Clearly the analysis of a single case limits both the strength and the range of general or comparative arguments (Kennedy, 1979: 671; Yin 1981). Yet such a study precludes neither a delineation of the relevant attributes of the case on the basis of which it may be compared to other instances, nor an exploration of the theoretical problems it raises. Accordingly, let me say a few words about the actual case chosen, and why it is suitable for the analysis of the questions I have set out to explore.

While I present a detailed description of the battalion in a later chapter, I note here that organizationally and socially it is very similar to other elite infantry units in Israel. The hundreds of men who make up the battalion are divided (as is typical in the IDF) into three rifle companies, one support company, and one headquarters company. According to IDF policy, each time the battalion is mobilized to perform missions assigned to it, it does so as one distinct organization. Moreover, it carries out the same operational tasks (in the occupied territories and along Israel's northern borders) and is subject to identical training stints and exercises as other elite infantry elements of the reserves. The battalion is characterized by roughly the same type of officer-men ratio, staffing practices, and allocation of personnel as other such combat units. Along these lines, we can safely assume a basic commonality of attributes between this unit and other such infantry battalions. This contention does not imply that there are no differences between the battalion and other units within and outside of the IDF. Rather it suggests that the case at hand forms a rough model through which to explore the issues I have set out for analysis and a case with which we can compare other military forces.[6]

A final issue is related to the ongoing struggle within academia about research methods. While some of my anthropological colleagues may see this as a weakness (a veritable "surrender" to supporters of the harder methodologies), I have intentionally incorporated explanations about my fieldwork (methods, observations and interpretations) into the text. I have done so for two reasons. One is the almost complete domination of studies of the military by psychologists, social psychologists, and sociologists who habitually use what are seen as hard methodologies (questionnaires, surveys, and experiments). It is out of respect for their outlook and out of a sensed need to engage them in constructive dialogue that I explicate my methodological biases. The other is that I believe that any piece of social research needs to clarify and explain its methods so that its findings can be appraised. Thus I have attempted to be careful about describing the advantages (and limits) of my research procedures (see also Appendix I).

Reading This Book

Let me offer a short synopsis of each chapter in order to orient prospective readers. The volume consists of nine chapters and nine interludes (or addenda) interspersed among them. The aim of these (at times rather light-hearted) interludes is to illuminate a number of points that are related to the daily circumstances of the battalion, and to more general characteristics of military life. Accordingly they serve to underscore a number of issues not directly related to, but nevertheless complementing, the main text.

In Chapter 2, I position my analysis in relation to contemporary scholarship devoted to the armed forces in general and to the Israeli army in particular. A classic debate in the sociology of the armed forces has revolved around the question of the uniqueness of the military: namely, whether military "professionalism" is similar to, or different from, the expertise found in other large-scale organizations. Taking off from contemporary scholarship I propose the existence of two kinds of professionalism within the military: one that is combat oriented or operational and another that is administrative and technical. The expertise and orientations of these two kinds of professionalism are two largely conflicting logics of organized collective action which are found in varying relative proportions in all components of military organization. I then suggest how a set of analytical tools borrowed from cognitive anthropology may help us in uncovering the folk models by which these "logics of action" are used by soldiers and officers as practical knowledge.

In Chapter 3, I move on to a description of the battalion in which I served and which forms the focus of my analysis. The purpose of this section is to familiarize readers without close knowledge of the IDF (or of military life in general) with some of the organizational and social characteristics of combat units. Readers familiar with the ongoing scholarship on the military (within and outside of Israel) and the reality of Israel's reserve service may skip Chapters 2 and 3 and proceed on the the next part of the text.

Chapter 4 is devoted to delineating the basic folk model of soldiering which centers on behavior in combat. This model (given the workings of human cognition, it is comprised of simple causal chains) is predicated on a combined image of soldiers-as-thinking-machines and a rhetoric of emotional control through which the performance of military missions is possible. The individual soldier is the juncture through which the elements of the model are expressed; he undertakes actions derived from membership in a machine-like organization, under extremely stressful circumstances, and masters emotions caused by the situation in order to carry out actions dictated by his commander.

In Chapter 5, I suggest that this model or schema serves as a "template" from which any number of propositions can be constructed. In the first section, I show how the model is used to evaluate, judge, or interpret the behavior of soldiers and officers in three domains: to appraise the professionalism of "ordinary" soldiers, to gauge the ability of officers to carry out military missions, and to evaluate the similarity of exercises and maneuvers to real combat situations. The second section of this chapter provides an opportunity to deal more explicitly with the comparative aspects of my case. I deal with the extent to which the model of combat is characteristic of other field units of the IDF (primarily other infantry detachments and the armored corps).

Chapter 6 deals with the kinds of images and notions that the men in the battalion have of enemies. The first section of the chapter is devoted to three issues: a "folk" categorization of enemies which is based on their perceived threat to survival; the manner by which opposing forces are depersonalized and objectified; and the discourse of emotional control which saturates talk about relations with enemy civilians. The second section comprises a comparison of the Israeli case with the American examples of the Second World War and the Vietnam War. I suggest that the process of depersonalizing enemies that is intrinsic to the combat model actually involves differing patterns of objectification (the enemy-as-object) as found in the IDF, and demonization (the enemy-as-demon) as found in the American ground forces.

Chapter 7 takes the examination of the combat model in a different direction. My contention is that if we are to gain a full understanding of military life, then we cannot be content with sketching the main schema of soldiering. We need to explain how this model is said to be internalized and then govern behavior in subsequent situations. Thus here I examine two major 'folk' models of motivation that characterize the men of the battalion: a causal chain predicating individual need-fulfillment which serves to explain and justify why commanders (usually officers) serve in the battalion; and one predicating the creation of an "atmosphere" of solidarity among troops so that they serve willingly and effectively.

Chapter 8 is my most speculative. Here I attempt to go beyond my case study's focus on cognitive models to wider issues related to military service and Israeli society. First, I suggest a number of ways in which emotional control within the army is linked to such mastery outside of it. Second, I propose how the combat schema may be associated with certain ideals of manhood among (Jewish) Israelis. To the best of my knowledge, apart from rather scattered remarks no systematic work on the link between military service and masculinity or notions of manhood has been carried out in Israel. Thus the suggestions in this chapter should be seen as just that, a series of conjectures and hypotheses for further investigation into these themes.

While I recapitulate the main themes explored in previous chapters in the volume's conclusion, in the Epilogue I return to examine a few more issues related to my own historical situatedness and its implications for an anthropology of the military.

NOTES

1. Associated terms are implicit theories or everyday or common-sense conceptions (Furnham 1987: 214).
2. By "elite" I refer to units that are formally recognized by the IDF as superior forces in terms of training, equipment and personnel and in terms of the kinds of missions they are assigned. To use an analogy, by elite forces I refer to Israel's equivalent of the 82nd Airborne and not to the variety of special forces found in the U.S. military (Simons 1997).

3. The Haganah was the main military organization of the prestate Jewish entity in Palestine, while the Palmach was its elite strike force.

4. In addition, the interest that Israel has excited in the social sciences and humanities is related to its wider historical context of protracted conflict and to the attendant scholarship which has attempted to come to terms with the social implications of this situation. Interestingly, while the case of Israel has had very little impact on the construction of general social theory (unlike the case of the USSR or Japan, for instance) it has had a respectable effect on the construction of theoretical approaches to a broad area of research called "armed forces and society." It is not coincidental that works dealing with comparative issues, or with the military in general, or with that broad field termed "armed forces and society" have invariably referred to the Israeli case (Schiff 1985). For example, in his overview of military psychiatry, Gabriel (1987) uses the Israeli case as one of a small number of instances in formulating his assessment of the history and present status of this discipline (see Ben-Ari and Lomsky-Feder forthcoming).

5. This point has been sorely missed by many students of the armed forces. Reserve soldiers are not passive "recipients" of socialization by members of the permanent forces who train them. They are often themselves quite active socialization agents for regulars (Ronen 1993).

6. Against this background, my analysis should be seen as what Yin (1981: 47-48) terms an exploratory case study, i.e. a single case design that is justified because it serves a revelatory purpose. It serves this purpose in three interrelated senses: by offering insights into a hitherto little explored set of questions (the folk models of soldiering); suggesting a novel approach to the military (an anthropological analysis); and, in suggesting further topics for analysis.

Interlude 1: The Tenor of Military Language

*M*ilitary language contains its own specific usages. This language allows, at one and the same time, the management of complex, large-scale organizations in a relatively efficient manner and the neutralization of often horrifying actions and experiences. The following expressions are taken from *The Facts on File Dictionary of Military Science* (compiled by Jay M. Shafritz, Todd J.A. Shafritz and David B. Robertson, 1989) and pertain to the armed forces of the English-speaking countries. In presenting these phrases my aim is not to provide readers with a glossary of terms used in my text, but rather to grant them a taste of this dual quality of professional military language.

Activate: To put into existence by official order a unit, post, camp, station, base or shore activity that has previously been constituted and designated by name or number, or both, so that it can be organized to function in its assigned capacity.

Adjutant: An officer acting as the chief administrative assistant to a unit commander. Usually only units of the battalion or regimental level have adjutants. In the British Army, the adjutant is also responsible for discipline among junior officers.

Area Fire: Fire delivered on a prescribed area. The term is applicable regardless of the tactical purpose of the fire, but area fire is usually neutralization fire.

Attack: An offensive action characterized by weapons fire and maneuvering, and culminating in a violent assault or, in an attack by fire, in delivery of intensive direct fire from an advantageous position. Its purpose is to direct a decisive blow to the enemy to hold him, destroy him in place, or force him to capitulate.

Battalion: A unit composed of a headquarters and two or more companies or batteries; anywhere between 300 to 1,000 soldiers. It is usually commanded by a lieutenant colonel and may be part of a regiment (or brigade) and may be charged with only tactical functions or it may be a separate unit and be charged with both administrative and tactical functions.

Battle Fatigue: A World War II term for mental exhaustion brought on by extended combat. Another term for the same phenomenon is combat-happy. Also called battle stress.

Buddy System: A system that requires two or more persons to work and remain near each other in certain areas and on certain missions so that they can give each other mutual protection and assistance. Often seen as the basis for development of unit morale.

Collecting Point: A place designated for the assembly of personnel, casualties, disabled materiel, salvage, and other items or persons for further movement to collecting stations or rear installations.

Combat Efficiency: The effectiveness of a force upon engaging the enemy; a unit that inflicted significant casualties on the enemy, while sustaining none of its own would be considered highly efficient, while a unit that merely traded casualties with the enemy is less so.

Combat Power: The total means of destructive or disruptive force that a military unit or formation can apply against an opponent at a given time.

Combat Troops: Those units or organizations whose primary mission is the destruction of enemy forces or installations.

Command and Control (C²): The exercise of authority and direction by properly designated commander over assigned forces in the accomplishment of a mission. Command and control functions are performed through an arrangement of personnel, equipment, communications, facilities, and procedures employed by a commander in planning, directing, coordinating, and controlling forces and operations in the accomplishment of the mission.

Company: The basic administrative and tactical unit most of arms and services of the U.S. Army. A company is on a command level below a battalion and above a platoon... A typical battalion will have three or four companies plus a headquarters company. Each company will typically contain four platoons.

Discipline: The unified obedience of a military unit, responsive to orders and adherence to military regulations. Without discipline, an army is no more than a mob.

Enemy Capabilities: The courses of action of which an enemy is physically capable. Enemy capabilities include not only the general course of action open to an enemy, such as attack, defense, or withdrawal, but also all the particular means possible to accomplish each general course of action. Enemy capabilities are considered in light of all known factors affecting military operations, including time, space, weather, terrain, and the strength and disposition of enemy forces.

Engagement: Any hostile encounter between opposing forces.

Fire Discipline: The ability to withhold fire until the enemy is close enough for the fire to be maximally effective.

Firepower: A measure of the amount of munitions (bullets, shells, mortar bombs, and other devices) that a military unit can deliver on a target. In the recent history of warfare, the concept of firepower has achieved increasing dominance, at the expense of maneuver, tactics, and even courage and morale... [Since World War I] all major armies equip their ordinary infantry with personal automatic weapons capable of firing hundreds of rounds a minute. Small squads carry portable antitank and antiaircraft weapons as powerful as the specialist weapons that would have been available only to the artillery units during World War II.

Infantry: The most basic branch of an army; those personnel and units who close with the enemy by means of fire and maneuver in order to destroy or capture him, or repel his assault by fire, close combat, and counterattack. Personnel and units so defined fight dismounted on foot or mounted according to the means of mobility provided. They are only provided with relatively light weapons and must depend on armor and artillery support.

Kill: To destroy an enemy soldier, vehicle, or other entity.

Kill Assessment: The process of determining the percentage of an enemy that has been nullified (destroyed).

Mopping Up: The liquidation of remnants of enemy resistance in an area that has been surrounded or isolated, or through which units of a force have previously passed without eliminating all active resistance.

Morale: The level of psychological and emotional functioning of an individual or group with respect to sense of purpose, confidence, loyalty and ability to accomplish tasks.

Mortality Rate: The number of deaths occurring in a military force during a given period, per 1,000 strength. The rate is calculated by dividing the number of deaths that occur in a given period by the average strength of the force during the same period, and multiplying by 1,000.

Planning: The formal process of making decisions for the future of individuals and organizations. Military planning is usually done by a general staff or unit staff.

Standardization: The process (within military services and between allies) of developing concepts, doctrines, procedures, and designs to achieve and maintain the most effective levels of compatibility, interoperability, interchangeability, and commonality in the fields of operations, administration, and materiel.

1. THE MILITARY, ANTHROPOLOGY, AND ORGANIZATIONAL CULTURE

*T*o a surprising degree as much as war and military service are a significant part of Israeli life, published academic works on social and cultural aspects of the IDF (Israel Defence Forces) are still not very numerous (Lieblich 1989: 142). Studies of the Israeli army have, in ways resembling much of the research carried out in regard to the armed forces of other industrialized societies, been characterized by a preponderance of discussions placed at the macro level of analysis (Lissak 1984). These studies include for example, examinations of the relations between the military system and the economic sphere (Mintz 1976; Kleiman and Pedatzur 1991), the political arena (Peri 1981; Lissak 1984), or the social system (Horowitz and Kimmerling 1974; Kimmerling 1984). Additional works that fall within this kind of approach include appraisals of policy making or historical reviews (Gabriel 1984; Luttwak and Horowitz 1975; Rothberg 1979; Wald 1992).

Research carried out on the micro level has tended to focus on the individual soldier (or on his attributes) from what are essentially psychological or social-psychological perspectives. These studies include such interrelated topics as motivation (Gal 1986: chap 4), perception (Shalit 1988), combat effectiveness (Amir 1969; Shirom 1976), leadership (Gal 1986: chap 7), or cohesiveness (Greenbaum 1979). Closely related to this literature are reports which deal with the treatment of stress or breakdown from the perspective of clinical psychology (Breznitz 1983; Milgram 1986).

Since the 1980s, however, a new set of approaches associated with cultural studies has raised questions about the place of the military and militarism in Israeli society. One set of inquiries has centered on the place of military symbols in various national rituals (such as Independence Day ceremonies) (Liebman and Don-Yehiye 1983; Handelman and Katz 1995; Handelman and Shamgar-Handelman 1997; Dominguez 1989). Other studies have highlighted mechanisms like public rites, literary texts, educational curricula, or linguistic usages by which collective meanings and memories related to "security" are transmitted and imparted in Israeli institutional life (Kalderon 1988; Meiron 1992; Melman 1993; Ofrat 1991, 1994; Veiler 1991). These investigations have often been expressions or adoptions of intellectual developments outside of Israel. In this respect, perhaps the most famous examples are the studies of Paul Fussel (1975; 1989) who examined the canonical and non-canonical literary works by which war is sacrilized and constructed in terms of collective memories. Within the social sciences we find works carried out by Kertzer (1988) on political rituals or Mosse (1990) on military cemeteries.

A related set of studies bears a greater affinity to my study. These inquiries have uncovered the processes and mechanisms by which a specific kind of militarism has been produced and reproduced in Israel. These studies have dealt with such issues as the historical developments by which military thinking has come to dominate politics (Ben-Eliezer 1995a, 1995b), the centrality of security and military considerations in policy making (Kimmerling 1993), and the manner by which the Israeli-Arab conflict has shaped the very subjects of academic research (Ehrlich 1987). Broadly put, the stress within these examinations has been on exploring how war and conflict are related to society. These scholars began their examinations by asking how war is an integral consideration of state institutions as they impinge on the larger society (Kimmerling 1984, 1985).[1] The major intellectual influences on these scholars have come from critical sociologists who have proposed that modern war is one of the primary means by which the state establishes its power within society by mobilizing resources for external conflicts. The most compelling argument of these sociologists has been to show how war (or its possibility) works towards centralizing the state and contributing to the institutionalization of the means of violence in a given society (Giddens 1985; Shaw 1988; Tilly 1985).

Thus while the first set of studies that began in the 1980s dealt with cultural constructions and collective representations, the second set dealt with how the Israeli state is dominated by security concerns. While the major contribution of the first group has been to highlight how major military symbols are promulgated in Israeli culture, the second group has offered insights into how Israel has become a society characterized by a certain kind of militarism and its resulting inequalities. Both sets of approaches, however, have tended to ask relatively few questions about what happens *within* the military. Here however, a series of studies rooted primarily in psychology and sociology have begun to ask different questions about the internal dimensions of Israel's armed forces. These works – like some very exceptional essays written in the 1970s (Schild 1973, or Gal 1973) – all focus on the "meanings," "purposes," or "intentions" that are related to military duties. Let me briefly comment about a number of these works in order to show how suggestive they are in methodological and analytical terms, and to use them as a means of formulating the main thrust of my analysis.

The first project is a book by Reuven Gal (1986) a former chief psychologist of the IDF. While still celebratory and quite laudatory of the Israeli army, it includes very good chapters on such issues as heroism and the "spirit" of combat units. Gal was the first to suggest systematically that it would be fruitful, for example, to explore how certain Israeli (Jewish male) propensities for initiative and gregariousness are inculcated by, and used within, the army. The second study is a book by developmental psychologist Amia Lieblich that focuses on transitions to adulthood that Israeli (Jewish) men undergo during their compulsory three or four years of service (1989; also Lieblich and Perlow 1988). Through an intriguing use of oral life histories, Lieblich underscores how the military "forges" men by letting them undertake a variety of highly responsible jobs in the context of disciplined and circumscribed units.

The third project germinated out of a Ph.D. thesis written by Sarit Helman at the Department of Sociology and Anthropology of the Hebrew University. Using a highly ingenious approach, Helman (1992) takes as the subjects of her analysis conscientious objectors to the war in Lebanon. Through analyzing the in-depth interviews she held with these rather marginal, but nevertheless highly perceptive men, she uncovered the types of discourse underlying war, peace, citizenship, and military service in Israel (propagated by active soldiers). A closely related work is the project carried out by Liebes and Blum-Kulka (1994) on the moral quandaries of soldiers that served in the Intifada (the Palestinian Uprising). Both ventures have served to highlight the manner by which meanings are created and managed by men serving within the military.

17

Other studies which should be mentioned in this regard include investigations into military funerals carried out by Nissan Rubin (1985). In this study, Rubin depicts the unofficial memorial rites carried out by one unit and thus raises the issue of how military organizations create and maintain a sense of a shared past. The final study is Edna Lomsky-Feder's (1994) Ph.D. thesis on the life histories of veterans of the Yom Kippur War of 1973. In an earlier work, Lomsky-Feder (1992) analyzes how military service and the experience of combat figure in the way in which war has been "normalized" within and outside of the Israeli military.

Interestingly, many of the newer works carried out in regard to the armed forces of other advanced industrial societies seem to be going in these directions. Thus, for example, the studies appearing in the collection edited by Segal and Sinaiko (1986) have demonstrated not only the importance of a "bottom-up" approach to the analysis of military life but also the utility of studying hitherto relatively little explored areas such as socialization into military life, the different criteria by which soldiers appraise themselves and their service, or the creation within the armed forces of certain folk images and stereotypes. Other works have suggested the profitability of analyzing military training in symbolic or ritualistic terms (Eisenhart 1975; Shatan 1977). Finally Ingraham (1984) has shown most forcefully how a rich, qualitatively minded approach can provide a basis for analyzing the relations between individual identities, primary group dynamics, organizational rules, and military culture. Common to all of these works is the coupling of innovative qualitative methodologies with novel areas of research.

Yet the challenge still remains one of directing the insights and analytical tools provided by these newer approaches to the kind of study I am proposing. In other words, one must show how a stress on coupling qualitative field methods with a theoretical stress on the creation and management of meaning within the military can uncover the folk models by which soldiers make sense of their experiences. Let me get at this point by suggesting how we may benefit by formulating anew one of the most central controversies in the study of armed forces and society.

Multiple Orientations and the Military World View

A classic debate between Samuel Huntington (1957) and Morris Janowitz (1971) has fueled discussion about the basic character of the military for over three decades. Essentially, the debate revolved around the civilianization of the armed forces. The parameters of this argument were certain social and organizational developments in the postwar era. While Huntington emphasized the continuing importance of the "traditional" heroic warrior role, Janowitz' thesis was that after the Second World War, this role gave way to an ascendant managerial-technical role, and that military professionals had become similar to the professionals of large-scale, bureaucratic, non-military institutions (see Harries-Jenkins and Moskos 1981: 11). In place of the static model of the armed forces as characterized by a radically different professionalism which was propounded by Huntington, Janowitz proposed a more dynamic one stressing the emergence of a pragmatic orientation in the military. Among the changes that led to the new orientation were technological developments, shifts in the number of staff, support and technical soldiers deployed (often formulated as the teeth-to-tail ratio), and the similarity of the military to civilian institutions (in terms of careering or authority relations, for example).

Janowitz, however, hastened to add that the convergence he described and analyzed would never be total. As he and a long line of other scholars well realized, the organized use of legitimate violence remains a type of human activity unlike any other; not even the impact of technology could succeed in making the conduct of war a purely technical set of tasks (Boene 1990: 21). Later, Janowitz began to talk of the military profession as consisting of a "mixture" of professional orientations: heroic leaders, military managers, and technical specialists. Indeed, in his words, any "one officer can come to embody various mixtures of these elements" (Janowitz 1971: xiii).

But by formulating a thesis based on a "mixture" of orientations Janowitz raised other questions: What does this "mixture" consist of? How, for example, is an individual soldier's (or commander's) diverse set of expertise – of managerial know-how, of what it is to be heroic, or of technical proficiency – interrelated? In the past two decades, scholars have offered a range of answers to such questions. Rather than undertake a full-scale review of this literature, I will outline three approaches as a context for the analytical thrust of my analysis.

The first, quite influential, approach has been proposed by Moskos (cited in Harries-Jenkins and Moskos 1981: 17ff.). His thesis revolves around a complex and dialectical movement of different parts of the armed forces towards or away from civilian society. The resulting model is thus not one based on polarization in which the military profession is or is not like civilian ones, but is "segmented" or "pluralistic"; at any one point some parts are like and others different from civilian society. For example, given the propagation of a heroic self-image combat units diverge from and administrative units converge toward the civilian sector. Two major criticisms have been directed toward this model (Harries-Jenkins and Moskos 1981: 17–18). The first is that the model seems to predicate the creation of two military institutions: one elitist and militaristic, and one popular and civilianized. The second criticism is that in practice it is impossible to break down integrated military units into distinct, delineated segments, each of which has its own orientations.

The second approach is exemplified in a later paper written by Harries-Jenkins (1986). While his specific empirical focus is on enlisted men in the British army, it is his analytical suggestions that interest us here. Harries-Jenkins begins his analysis from the realization that both the older center (combat units) and periphery (support units) model of the military, and Moskos' segmented military model rightly emphasize the heterogeneous nature of the military. Yet he offers an interesting way of conceptualizing this heterogeneity. He suggests that we differentiate between two sets of criteria that underlie conceptions of the army: "pull" factors for joining the military which include different role-images like warrior, worker and technician; and "push" factors, which are less ideal but practical attitudes regarding what can be achieved within military service (career development for instance). The advantages of this approach lie not only in heightening our awareness of the internal differentiation within the British – or for that matter any – military, but no less importantly in underscoring the diverse ideal images and practical attitudes that govern the way military life is described or evaluated. However, this approach leaves unexplained the organization of "mixtures" of images and attitudes in specific units or in individual soldiers, and the manner by which these images and attitudes are played out in the concrete reality of military life.

The third approach, developed by Hubert Jean-Pierre Thomas and taken up by Boene (1990: 24ff.), represents an attempt to deal with some of these problems. The thrust of their argument is the necessity of moving beyond the theoretical divergence/convergence debate. The hypothesis Thomas raises is the existence of two subsystems that are functionally and culturally -*not* structurally – distinct: the combat-oriented or operational subsystem and the administrative-technical subsystem. The objective of the combat oriented subsystem is to execute combat related missions and the role model is that of warrior. The administrative-technical subsystem is instrumental in nature, the technical division of labor is important, and the role models are workers, technicians and managers.

> Since they are not to be equated with surface structural features, it is futile to search for physical boundaries between them: they are two largely conflicting logics of organized collective action, to be found in varying relative proportions in all components of military organization and all situations. In other words, their relationship is one of dialectical tension: the full expression or incarnation of one logic is necessarily frustrated by the inescapable presence of the other. (Boene 1990: 25)

This is, to say the least, an innovative way of thinking about the military, for here we find the notion that military uniqueness may reside in a duality of subjective orientations and dialectically related organizational patterns of rationality and internal legitimacy (Boene 1990: 26). Furthermore, the conceptualization of different "logics of action" lets us ask different questions of military organization: first, because it cautions us to cease looking for some kind of essential connection between particular orientations and specific physical persons or units; and second, because this conceptualization leads us to see as problematical the co-existence in a state of tension of a number of conflicting orientations and ways of thinking inside peoples' heads.[2]

Anthropology, Meaning Systems and Folk Models

But how are these "logics of action" organized as practical knowledge? What methodology can best uncover and explicate the different reasonings attendant on military actions? The line of research that I outlined in the first part of this chapter seems to be suggestive in this respect. These approaches to the study of military meaning systems prod us to examine the manner by which military knowledge is internally organized and used for practical purposes. A specifically anthropological perspective may help us delineate the precise kinds of tools needed to uncover these meanings.

The study of cultures or "meaning systems" has long been one of the primary subjects of anthropological inquiry. Contemporary anthropology offers an array of analytical approaches to the study of culture. Yet there seem to be three underlying issues which any convincing approach to the analysis of meaning systems must be able to address (Quinn and Holland 1987: 3–4): (1) the apparent systematicity of cultural knowledge, or how a certain culture is characterized and distinguished from others by certain central themes; (2) the internal organization of complex meaning systems, or how humans come to master the enormous amount of knowledge that they have of the world; and (3) the generative capacity of cultural knowledge, or how this (essentially practical) knowledge is extended to new or novel situations. One innovative approach which I have adopted here, may be fruitful in helping us to grapple with these issues as they are related to the military.

Cognitive anthropology, as this approach is labeled, began its inquiries by pursuing the question of what one needs to know in order to behave as a functioning member of one's society or social group. This school of thought came to stand for a view of culture as "shared knowledge" which is not a people's general customs and artifacts or received oral traditions, but what they must *know* in order to act as they do, make things they make, and interpret their experiences in distinctive ways (Quinn and Holland 1987: 4; D'Andrade 1995). Since the early 1980s, cognitive anthropology has begun to systematically inquire about "cultural" or "folk" models: the taken-for-granted models of the world that are widely shared by members of a social group (although not necessarily to the exclusion of alternative models) and that represent and explain the way the "world" (or parts of the world) is ordered. The term "folk" does not imply that these models are adhered to by the untutored masses, but suggests their common sense nature and the fact that they characterize a certain organization or group of people. These models, which predicate certain simplified causal chains and may be marked by internal contradictions, serve practical purposes: they figure in the way people describe, explain, or justify such things as their tangible surroundings, the probable outcomes of behavior, and their ongoing experiences (Keesing 1987: 374).

In more abstract terms, a folk model or schema is a distinct and strongly interconnected pattern of interpretive elements that can be activated with minimum inputs. A schema is an interpretation that is frequent, well organized, memorable, and can be made from minimal cues, contains one or more prototypic instantiations, and is relatively resistant to change (D'Andrade 1992: 29). The import of this conceptualization is that it goes beyond the stress on abstract values, attitudes, or orientations to put at the center of scholarly attention the sets of causal schemes and actable forms people learn.

Accordingly, I suggest that an examination of the "folk" models – the logics of action, reasonings, and propositions – that officers and soldiers use in order to "make sense" of what they do and who they are, may be a good entryway into the meaning "soldiering" holds for them. Furthermore, I propose that this kind of analysis may lead us to understand how concepts like "conflict", "force," or "the enemy" are related to the ongoing actions of troops and commanders. To reiterate the proposal I put forward in the Introduction, the aim of this project is to reconstruct the practical cultural understandings of military life in the infantry battalion I have singled out for analysis. In terms of the issues set out in this chapter, such a move will allow us to relate the discussion found in the scholarly literature about the armed forces to the specific context of the IDF.

I now turn to a brief description of the unit.

NOTES

1. Thus for example, people such as Yuval-Davis and Kimmerling have linked military service to patterns of gender, power and inequality. Yuval-Davis' (1987) scheme centers on the divergence found in the Israeli army (as in all armies) between roles found at the "front" and at the "rear." She shows how these two kinds of army roles have historically developed into a pattern of sexual division of labor: the men are at the front in combat related roles, and the women are at the back staffing support roles (both within the military and outside it). Kimmerling (1993: 217) for his part, suggested that the military itself is basically a macho and male-oriented subculture. The result has been the marginalization – through the military – of Jewish-Israeli women throughout society. The overall impact of this situation has been not only the reinforcement of women's general marginality, but also their exclusion from the most important societal discourse in Israel, that of "national security".

2. Parenthetically, it should be stated that this is still a rather synchronic model and that a full-fledged analysis would take into account both Moskos's and Harries-Jenkins's stress on understanding the historical circumstances surrounding the development of any model of the military.

INTERLUDE 2:
CAMARADERIE AND
FELLOWSHIP

❧❧❧

*O*n the morning of the day we were to complete an operational deployment in the occupied territories, I wrote the following in my field journal.

Last night all of the companies held parties. In the headquarters company the party consisted of a festive meal that the cooks had prepared: hamburgers and french fries. I remember thinking that the five salads they also served taught me something about a positive correlation between the number of salads served at an Israeli party and its festiveness. About forty of us converged on the dining hall and to the accompaniment of an accordion (a member of a nearby [religious] settlement volunteers to play for every unit serving in the area) we sang shira-betzibur (sing-alongs). We sang what are known as songs of Eretz Ysrael, songs of the land of Israel: a core of well-known Hebrew songs. One of the helpers to the battalion's sergeant major sang a Yemenite song while the rest of us sang a refrain. Despite singing off-key he was well received with much whooping and hand clapping. The party was over after the meal and some of the men continued to their own smaller parties: the communications men, the cooks with the quartermaster's clerks.

I was also invited to A company. As in other companies a few shekel were gathered from each of the men, and with the money the company sergeant major and the clerk bought meat, hummus and pita bread for a barbecue. These were served in combination with the food provided by the army. While the party was held to signal the end of the deployment stint it was combined with a party to say goodbye to the former company commander who had become deputy commander of the battalion, the former sergeant major who had become an assistant to the operations officer, the former clerk who had moved to be one of my assistants, and a few other soldiers who had moved to administrative roles in the headquarters unit.

Apart from the food, two soldiers had prepared a humorous skit about the company's main "characters." The skit included some fun poked at the present company commander who rarely smiles. The soldiers who had left the company received small mementos: shields with the names and symbols of the IDF, the infantry division, and our specific unit.

During the festivities which lasted for about three hours the conversation began with chit-chat and small talk but as the evening wore on some lively conversation ensued. The conversation began to jump from one topic to another with no apparent linking theme; topics were taken up at the whim of each speaker and in rapid succession. Soon the jokes and jibes turned to poking fun of various men and usually prompted immediate boisterous laughter.

In addition, it was arranged that during the party the men constantly rotated so that those who were on duty could also participate.

***

The following are excerpts from an interview with a former NCO of C company who had moved on to become a clerk. He was in his late thirties and a musician and music teacher. We sat in the commander's office (which was available for a few hours) and began talking of the kinds of ties that are created in the army.

Q: *Many soldiers say that they like being in a company; do you agree?*
A: *Yes that's where you are with people that you are with in operational deployment and in training and there you really find that ties are created. And if I think of ties that have been created during reserve duty, then these deeper ties were with people that I was with during these periods; these periods of operational deployment and being in frontline posts (mutsavim).*

Q: *When you say ties, do you mean that you see these people outside the army?*
A: *Outside the army? No, I don't have these kinds of ties. But if I meet them outside the army then you have some kind of feeling of a tie. Take Jacob; the fact that we spent so much time together and talked about all sorts of things; well, it creates a sort of feeling that we have a tie between us....*
These are people that you spend time with, hours and hours: you sleep with them, eat with them; and then you go out on activities with them and they lend you a helping hand; and especially when you are in pressured situations. Then you learn about them and learn to respect them. Especially you discover, like in Lebanon, that someone whom you thought was a problem, then he suddenly is

someone who is very positive during a difficult period. When you are with people in a pressured time then it creates....

Q: *Didn't it ever bother you that you didn't meet these people outside the army?*
A: *No, not especially. But only once. We had a party in Jaffa after the first period in Lebanon. As I told you, this was the hardest period ever in reserves. And we were there in Lebanon for a month and I remember that the first two weeks passed by like a day because of the tension. It was there that we participated in a battle with tanks shooting, and artillery and whole buildings fell. And then the party was an outcome of the feeling that we had; that we wanted to meet and to be together. I really expected that we would feel like one unit, like being all together. But then it was strange because I didn't feel that I was like part of one whole unit. I felt close to some of the people there but not to everyone. It was to the people I had something to say to that I felt close; the people that I could talk to about all sorts of things like politics....*

Now there are other people that you like because they're nice people but not because you can talk to them. They are nice and helpful and positive but sometimes you don't have much to talk to them about. But when I think about it I would rather have them in the company than someone who is an intellectual but with whom I don't have much to talk about.

2. THE UNIT:
AN INFANTRY BATTALION

*A*ccording both to official designations and to the self-perception of the men, the unit belongs (with a number of other battalions) to one of the army's select infantry brigades. It is distinguished, to put this by way of the abstraction and preciseness which characterizes military parlance, by a high level of readiness and combat effectiveness. This classification implies that it is allocated significant combat and operational missions, and that it is interchangeable with other high quality battalions of the IDF. Yet it is an organization that is made up exclusively of reservists, of *miluim-niks* (literally, "people who fill in the gap"). These soldiers and officers volunteered for one of the "crack" infantry forces during their compulsory term of service and upon completion of that term were assigned to our unit. Thus, the bulk of the troops (including a majority of the administrative soldiers) have served in the Golani, Givati, or Nahal Brigades of the IDF's standing or regular forces.

The reserve system is the largest component of the IDF, and its establishment and maintenance are aimed at solving the manpower problems of a relatively small population facing a situation of protracted conflict (Gal 1986). In addition, this system furnishes an efficient solution both for sustaining a highly trained and accessible military force (that can be mobilized quickly in emergencies) and for allowing the continuation of "normal" life when the conflict is relatively placid. By law every man who has completed his compulsory service (between three and four years) can be mobilized until the age of 50 for a yearly stint of up to 42 days. In reality, units like our battalion are usually called up twice a year and often for longer periods. As in other parts of the army the burden shouldered by officers and senior NCOs (non-commissioned officers) is considerably greater than that of lower-ranking soldiers (Gal 1986:40). The former are continuously involved in such activities as briefings, staff meetings, additional training, or tactical tours. During the seven years that I was in the unit I served (apart from one-day or half-day assignments) for a total of 340 days.

As is typical in the IDF, the few hundred men of the battalion are divided into five companies. While the commander of the unit holds the rank of lieutenant-colonel, the commanders of the five companies usually have the rank of captain or major. The three rifle companies are the main combat components of the battalion and each is made up of platoons of infantry soldiers (normally commanded by lieutenants) and small support and administrative detachments. The support company is in charge of handling the battalion's more substantial support weapons (essentially mortars and antitank missiles) and its scouting functions. The headquarters company includes the unit's commander and his deputy, and various elements such as communications, operations, intelligence, medicine, and personnel, ordnance, and munitions. Like all such reserve units in the Israeli Army (including the armored corps and the artillery), the battalion is composed exclusively of men. The small number of women who serve in the IDF's field units in effect do so in the standing or permanent forces.

The battalion, to use a term often used in the IDF, is an "organic" unit (*yechida organit*). Organizationally, this term implies first that, like other such units, it is first a framework characterized by a permanent membership and structure of roles, and second that upon mobilization the whole battalion (as one complete organized entity) is recruited. The logic at base of this organizational arrangement is that it allows the easy replacement and rotation of units with similar capabilities (Gal 1986: 41). Internally, this arrangement implies that there is a stability of personnel and a continuity of operating and commanding styles which lead to reliability of expectations and behavior. The unit trains at least once a year and its commanders are proud of the high level of competence shown during these maneuvers. While the battalion carries out a variety of military tasks, during the last few years it has been deployed along Israel's northern borders and in the Intifada.

In an infantry battalion, soldiers tend to be younger than the men found in equivalent fighting units of the armored corps or the artillery.

The fact that many of the missions and tasks assigned to the unit require quite intense physical activity means that at about the age of thirty or so, most of the regular soldiers are shifted out to units populated by older troops while a small number move within the battalion to the head-quarters company. Thus many of the unit's clerks, cooks, mechanics and drivers are ex-combat soldiers. From the commanders' point of view these men are of considerable value: they are familiar with the combat drills and the types of tasks assigned to the infantry, can fire a variety of weapons should they be called upon to do so, and are accustomed to the sometimes harsh conditions under which the unit operates.

Socially, the term "organic" unit implies a military force characterized by relatively high cohesion, overlapping primary groups and a certain sense of a shared past. Like many reserve units in the IDF, and in contrast to many Western armies (for example, Simons 1997), the general atmosphere in the battalion tends towards the informal and the familiar. While there is a clear demarcation between officers (or senior NCOs filling officer roles) and the rest of the men, rank is relatively de-emphasized (Levin and Halevy 1983: 17). For example, everyone (including the unit's commander) is called by a given name (or equivalent nicknames). All soldiers and officers serve under similar general conditions; they have the same beds and barracks, the same food and canteen services, similar clothes and equipment, and approximately the same kind of furloughs.

This relative egalitarianism is all the more notable since the battalion is socially quite heterogeneous. It is diverse both in terms of Jewish ethnic groupings (more than half of the soldiers and officers are from Middle Eastern backgrounds) and religious affiliation (it has a sizable group of observant Jews). Occupationally, the men come from a variety of walks of life: students and garage mechanics, managers and store owners, farmers and lawyers, government clerks and salesmen, shopkeepers and electricians, and house painters and technicians.

As in all of the IDF's reserve units, a variety of informal activities form the social glue linking the unit's soldiers together. Stories, anecdotes, and (sometimes) "tall" tales are constantly told and retold in a variety of groupings. Favorite subjects include combat experiences in Lebanon, episodes from the men's compulsory term of service, stints of training throughout the country, and periods of reserve duty in the Intifada or along the borders facing Syria and Lebanon. As is common in all-male groups, a good deal of banter accompanies almost all activities: people tell dirty jokes, play practical gags on each other, and constantly tease one another verbally and physically.

Favorite activities are coffee sessions usually marked by witticisms, the spread of rumors, gossip about members of the unit, discussions about the "distributive justice" of duties and furloughs, and backgammon and domino games. Conversations at these gatherings often focus on "civilian" matters such as people's jobs and businesses, the stock market and finance, trips and vacations within and outside of Israel, or movies and music. During periods of deployment (but never during training) the men watch sports and news on television or pornographic movies. Reserve duty, however, is not a period of total disconnection from "civilian life" (*ha-ezrachoot*); people constantly talk to their families and friends, and many people maintain frequent, even daily, contact with their workplaces by means of cellular phones.

As for my own role, as a staff officer, the adjutant (*shalish*) of the battalion, I was in charge of various matters such as human resources, helping the battalion commander issue orders, mobilizing and demobilizing the whole unit, or dealing with soldiers who had "gone" AWOL and promotions. With the exception of my last period of duty, I held the rank of captain. I am now a major and have been reassigned to a post in one of the army's behavioral sciences units.

INTERLUDE 3:
ACTION, FEAR,
AND FIGHTING MEN

Are You Nervous in the Service?

Are you nervous in the service Mr. Jervis?
Do you wish that you were anywhere but here?
As the shells begin a-squealing
Do you get that empty feeling
That your life has been shortened by a year?...
Are you nervous in the service Mr. Jervis?
Are you frantic — don't know quite what to do?
Well, please don't let it getcha,
For you'll find, if time will letcha,
That, though you're nervous, I am nervous too.

Eddie Bendityky, Private,

(U.S. Army's official newspaper during the Second World War: *The Stars and Stripes*).

***

The following passages are taken from an interview with a driver, in his mid-thirties, who had been a driver for all of his military life. We held our conversation in the infirmary, one quiet spot where we would not be constantly interrupted.

Q: *Did you ever think of being a fighter* (lochem)*?*
A: *Well from the beginning I wanted to be a driver. But I am a fighter. In reality, I am a fighter. We in this battalion are all fighters and we participate in patrols and in penetrations [into enemy territory] on APCs [armored personnel carriers]. We carry the troops and we also shoot if we have to. That means we [drivers] are people you can depend on.*

Q: *But don't you feel sometimes that the other people look down on drivers?*
A: *Yes, well at the beginning I thought that, but since I began to be with the fighters I saw that there is no difference. In my compulsory term of service and here as well, in this unit of reservists, there are no differences. Someone told me that in the old days there were these drivers with big bellies and in sorts of cliques, but all that's gone now. We are like the rest of the soldiers.*

In fact we are even spoiled a bit. Everyone understands that we work hard, long hours. Especially here during operational deployment we work six hours and then rest six hours and so on. Sometimes they ask us to work even more.

3. A MODEL OF COMBAT: SOLDIERING AND EMOTIONAL CONTROL

Soldiers are the tradesmen of killing, but officers are the managers of violence.
Harold Lasswell

*L*et me begin with a not untypical passage from a conversation I had with Ehud, commander of one of the rifle companies, and one of the most eloquent and articulate of the unit's officers. Speaking of what he had undergone in Lebanon as a commander of the mortar platoon, he recalled:

> At that period I reached the apex of my competence in terms of activating six [mortar] barrels under conditions of pressure, night after night. Really, with successful hits, really excellent hits. And from that moment I went down in terms of my professional ability, in terms of the tension, in terms of everything.

While very brief, this passage includes many of the main elements we associate with soldiering and commanding in combat; including professional competence, composure under fire, fulfillment of assigned tasks, and the firefight as the essence of military service. How does such an officer formulate this kind of statement? And conversely, how do we as listeners or readers understand the meaning of such texts?

My argument here is threefold: first, that soldiers like Ehud formulate such accounts based on a basic set of cultural or folk understandings about military life; second, that while such basic understandings may actually be very complex, given the workings of human cognition they are formulated on the basis of a set of rather simple causal chains or of a model of soldiering; and third, that this model may be uncovered through a focus on the images and metaphors – that is, the likenesses, suggestive resemblances, and representations – that soldiers use in order to talk about military service. Accordingly, I begin with the three central clusters of metaphors that are used in this Israeli battalion to talk about military units. For anyone familiar with the military it will be readily apparent that these metaphors are similar to the ones used in frontline units of other armies. While I think that there are features which are unique to the IDF, I leave an explication of these distinctive qualities for later.

The Unit (Battalion) as Machine

Not surprisingly, the dominant metaphors used by officers and soldiers to describe the battalion are related to machinery and to industrial production. This is not surprising, because analyses of the military have long underscored its claim to professional competence in the management of violence (Lang 1972:29; Shay 1995: 17). This claim alerts us to the fact that underlying much of modern military structures are certain "folk" notions of organization. The Israeli military, like all modern armies, is characterized by strong mechanistic assumptions and images: units of the armed forces are thought to operate and have the qualities of machines. But what does it mean that military units are likened to machines? What the metaphor of a machine – or its closely related image of an industrial factory – does is to ascribe the characteristics of a machine to a military unit (or to any other organization). Let me clarify this point through the following short excerpt from a three-hour interview I held with Yoel, a former commander of the battalion. We were talking about how he saw his role when he said:

> Your mission (*mesima*) is to build a framework that will be able to immediately undertake any task assigned to it and that it will perform that mission with a minimum of casualties. Your responsibility is that things will go smoothly in this framework and this would include the capability of one company commander to replace another. This means that there will be the smallest number of snags as possible in the way of the framework continuing to function as a framework.

In this short passage we can see quite a number of examples of this metaphorical mapping: the smoothness and efficiency of the unit's performance, the activation of the battalion, or the interchangeability of parts are all like similar qualities that we assume (or more correctly, know) that machines have. Likewise in the same interview, Yoel goes on to stress that different parts of the unit have different prices attached to them, again not unlike the different prices that parts of a machine have:

> I don't think it would be good for the battalion commander to be the first to go [get killed], because of the price this would entail. Not the moral price, but the price in terms of the functioning of the framework. When he goes the chance that the system will continue to go on working won't be very high.

When we talk of organizations as machines (Morgan 1986:22), we often have in mind a state of orderly (mechanical) relations between clearly defined parts that operate in a steady and productive manner. In analytical terms, the machine is the source domain, while the military unit is the target domain (Lakoff and Kovecses 1987:199). Because we usually have a more extensive knowledge of the source domain (in our case machines and factories), the use of the metaphor illuminates certain characteristics of the target domain (in our case the battalion).

Let me give other examples. Tasks undertaken by the services company were often referred to by the deputy battalion commander as "finished products," and one of the most popular expressions used by superiors is "give me the bottom line," as in a balance sheet or a business recommendation. Yet again, in appraising the caliber of soldiers it is not uncommon to hear of "product quality" or "product description," or of filling or emptying organizational slots as in "I need three marksmen," "I can still make use (*lehishtamesh*) of that soldier," or "I need three backs [to carry communications gadgets] during the exercise." Commanders often talk of having a squad or a platoon "in the clip/magazine" (*makhsanit*) to refer to a unit kept in readiness for an assigned mission. Correspondingly, in referring to himself before a combat patrol on the border with Lebanon one company commander said, half jokingly: "if I don't come out don't worry there are plenty of spare parts [*sper*, literally "spare tires"] around." Finally, during a training exercise the battalion commander was explicit about the replacement of one commander by the next should the first one be "finished."

In a related vein, the stress on coordinating and synchronizing units, actions and assignments is evident through the use of such devices as firing tables, task assignment programs, timetables, unit combat readiness and location tables, and definitions of missions and forces. The point to note in regard to all these kinds of lists and tables is the assumption that underlies their use: by expecting military units to work like machines, we expect them to operate in routinized, efficient, reliable, and predictable ways.

Other examples are linguistic usages found only in the army, and which implicitly posit a continuum or equivalence between people and machines. The first example is the verb "to operate" (*letaf'el*) that is employed in regard to light and heavy firearms and APCs (armored personnel carriers), as well as to individual soldiers or units (squads, teams, platoons, companies, or battalions). The second example is the term "combat readiness" (*kshirut mivtsa'it*), which again can be applied to equipment of various scales and complexities and to units comprised of human combatants. The third example is to talk of a unit in terms of the equipment it uses, as in the example of the kitchen orderly who told me, "I'm going to give the tanks breakfast," i.e. the tank crews who were training with one of our companies. These linguistic expressions can be used in a humorous vein. When talking about a deputy company commander who performed rather miserably in a training exercise, two NCOs referred to him as a "total loss," the term used by insurers to refer to the complete destruction of a car in traffic accident without the possibility of being put back into use.

The Unit as Bureaucracy

A closely related, yet analytically distinct, metaphor is that of the unit as a bureaucratic organization. Some men use not only terms like "system" or "framework" to talk about the battalion but also such expressions as "large firm," "business," "big plant," or simply "organization." The connotation of such imagery may be understood through the following three expressions often used by officers and NCOs. The first term is "to close matters" (*lisgor inyanim*) which carries with it the American English connotations of "connect," "secure," "finalize," or "make clear." It is employed in regard to finalizing plans, settling agreements, or checking that preparations for activities have been carried out. The second term is "definition" (*hagdara*) or "to define" (*lehagdir*). This expression is used when people want to emphasize the clear and specific contents of their expectations and requests (for instance, "give me a definition of what you want accomplished in the drills"). The third term is "procedures" (*nohalim*), which is used in regard to administrative responsibilities and communications programs as well as to combat related drills. In all three terms the undertone is one of clear and unambiguous messages about practical army tasks, and the emphasis is on clear categorization of actions, people, and things as a basis for action.

This metaphor differs from the machine metaphor in terms of the chunk of attributes it evokes. If the basic image of the machine metaphor is that of an automaton, the basic image of the bureaucratic metaphor is that of clerks carrying out clearly defined and circumscribed tasks. The bureaucratic imagery is of an organization based on fixed division of labor, hierarchical supervision, and detailed codes of instructions and regulations. These chunks of characteristics are not a set of Weberian ideal typical elements which can form the basis of a scientific analysis, but they do serve as a basis for the appraisal of the ongoing life of the unit and of military service.

In reality, the metaphors of machine and bureaucracy are often used in combination with little awareness of the differences between them. One often finds it hard to delineate which metaphor is being applied by soldiers and officers. Take the kind of connections made between communication and hierarchy and between equipment and men in the following text from an interview with Ehud, the previously cited commander of C company. We were discussing the ubiquitous term "professionalism" (*miktso'iyut*) in the army:

> There are two levels to a professional company. The first level is that of command... The line (*shdera*) of command, leading from me to the platoon commanders to the NCOs. Things do not run on their own, but are controlled, commands are given and performed according to directions that I give and I work according to the line of thought of the battalion commander... The other side is that of professional soldiering (*chayaloot*), how to enter a firing position (*emda*), how to enter a room, how to attack a fortified target, how to ride an APC – all of these things down to the simplest things.

Turn your attention first to the way Ehud uses the machine metaphor to talk of soldiering. Notice that he provides me with a list of techniques in which men, equipment, and drills are part of a single process. For readers not familiar with the army I should mention that a great deal of time is devoted to specific drills like the proper manner by which a team of two soldiers enter a room in which there may by enemy soldiers, or the correct manner by which one provides covering fire for attack. These drills involve set patterns of movement, specified uses of weapons, and fixed vocal reports of completion of the drills. Yoel, the former battalion commander, gave me an example of this singular men-equipment-drills process when we discussed soldiering. He said that the soldiers had done most drills hundreds of times and that by now they carried them out smoothly and efficiently. "Professional" soldiers according to this characterization, then, are expected to reach a high level of automaticity in carrying out certain drills.

Consider command next. It seems almost as though Ehud is talking of "driving" the company like a mechanical means of transportation but along a route dictated *to* him by the battalion's commander and dictated *by* him to the company. His image of the company is a compound of mechanics and bureaucracy: unity of command (beginning, of course, above him), a scalar chain (being the frame through which communication from top to bottom is effected), and a span of control which allows the coordination of all constituent units. In a similar vein, other officers address the constant necessity for supervision and control (*bakara*) in such military units. The connotation of these characterizations, however, is not always – if at all – that of a mindless use of machines, but rather, the regulation of the unit on the basis of clear lines of communication and strict rules and regulations.

To conclude this section then, the metaphors I have outlined offer composite images of efficiency and rationality (men, equipment, and drills), coordination and synchronization (times, places, and activities), and distinctions and categorizations (of units, authority structure, and regulations).

The Unit (Battalion) as Brain

Yet arguing that the primary metaphors used in regard to the unit are that of a machine (a mechanical instrument) or of a bureaucracy (an ordered division of labor) designed to carry out tasks, is still too simple. In the interview I held with Yoel (a highly successful director of a manufacturing firm), he often used other terms that, while grounded in the language of management, sounded somehow different. For example, he spoke of such matters as "acquiring managerial skills," "building a system of working relations," "managing the business," or of "management wisdom." I began to comprehend the significance of this terminology when we discussed the resemblance between running a business and commanding an army battalion:

> Now in terms of thinking and planning. In both places [business and the army] you make decisions; it's your role as commander or manager if you're looking for the commonalities. Now you can't plan anything if you can't define the situation, the conditions of the environment (*matsav hateva*). Now here you call it intelligence and there you call it market research. It's the same thing... Now it's true in the army, that you won't send someone [without real directions], sort of like "go over there, somewhere there is a *wadi* [a dry bed of a river]," so it's the same in business. Policymaking in both places is the same. You have to set the parameters: price, number of agents, advertising budget. In marketing these things are your ammunition. Now in the army you say; "Wait a minute what have I got here? Point targets? Area targets? Infantry? Armor?" You even choose the types of ammunition in the part called fire-plan.

In general terms, Yoel is talking about the relationship between an organization and its environment. More specifically, he is discussing the planning and reactive capacities of the battalion to uncertain and changing circumstances.

The reasoning underlying this passage may be clarified against the background of a pair of contrasting labels – one negative and the other positive – which are sometimes applied to soldiers and officers in the battalion (and throughout the IDF). The rather standard derogatory term is *rosh katan*, which literally means "small head" or "little head." Closely associated terms are the humorous "pin head" (*rosh sika*), "tweezers head" (*rosh pintseta*) implying a crown small enough to be picked up with tweezers, or "small-light-bulb head" (*rosh natznatz*). These terms usually refer to soldiers who are considered somewhat "lower-grade," whether mediocre, inept, or unwilling, and who lack motivation or are disillusioned with army life (see Lieblich and Perlow 1988: 44; Shalit 1988: 172; Feige and Ben-Ari 1991). From the point of view of commanders, the prime grievance against these soldiers is their unwillingness to take on responsibilities and their apathy (thus perhaps two English equivalents are soldiers who "lie low" or "keep a low profile"). Interestingly this negative label is a corollary of both the machine and the bureaucratic metaphors. If the image of "small head" is one of an automatic soldier unthinking and lacking initiative, the other is the clerk doing exactly what is in his job specification. One soldier who was rather proud of his "small head" put it this way: "What I know is only what interests me, and not all those things the decision makers sit there and talk about all day."

The contrasting category is one of *rosh gadol,* a big head, which is used to characterize people with initiative, drive and a sense of enterprise. Related terms include "open head" (*rosh patu'ach*), "open not square" (*patu'ach lo meruba*), "thinking" (*chashiva*), "imagination" (*dimyon*), "using one's head" (*haph'alat rosh*), "judgment" (*shikul da'at*), or "operating the brain" (*haph'alat moach*). The essential metaphor at work here, although it is not one used explicitly by the men, is of "unit as brain," or "unit as mind." By this assertion I mean the likening of certain military activities to the information processing and reactive capabilities of the human brain or mind (Morgan 1986:81).

The use of this metaphor is related to the limits of the machine image. The mechanistic approach is well suited to conditions characterized by straightforward tasks and a stable environment, i.e., circumstances in which machines and standardized bureaucracies work well (Morgan 1986:34). Conversely, it is restricted in terms of its adaptability and its potential for leading to "robotic" compliance or strict adherence to rules and regulations. Thus organizations which, like the army, need to be able to scan and sense changes in the environment, and to innovate and react to these changes are usually characterized by figures of speech related to the "braininess" or "mindfulness" of the organization (Dyer 1985: 135–3).[1]

Let us look at a number of examples of the "unit as brain" metaphor. The first instance is taken from an interview with Itai, the battalion's deputy commander. We were having a conversation about what he looks for in military service: "Where do the interesting things begin? When the field (*shetach*) creates problems that are unexpected, and you have to meet those problems with your own initiative." Corollaries of this view are found in expressions commanders use such as "creativity in managing," "problem solving," or "meeting challenges is like solving crossword puzzles." Moreover, when officers on all levels talked of accepting "smart comments" from soldiers they seemed to be stressing the need for a basic openness to suggestions about the operation of the unit in a changing environment.

One of the most common, if telling, phrases used to appraise troops and commanders is their "ability to think beyond their organizational slot or box (*mishbetset*)." This concise expression captures at one and the same time a desired ability to comprehend the general picture within which the unit is operating (i.e., the environment), to process information relevant to concrete action, and to act beyond the dictates of one's role (in the machine or in the bureaucracy). While I have very little comparative data on this point, I would suggest that to a greater degree than in other armies, the IDF's elite combat units encourage initiative down to the level of ordinary soldiers. One expects troops to be open and innovative to a greater degree than in other armed forces (Moshe Lissak, personal communication; Gal 1973; Gal 1986). Indeed, so prevalent is the stress on innovation that it has even led to the coining of the humorous phrase extensively used throughout the Israeli military, "Every plan is a basis for changes" (*kol tokhnit hi bassis leshinuim*).

This kind of "open headedness" of all troops is also evident in the constant stress on self-improvement and learning from mistakes in carrying out tasks (*lekakhim*). My diary is full of references to meetings at the end of training or operational deployment, short gatherings at the end of patrols, or conversations between soldiers in the barracks in which quality improvement is the central theme. During these formal and informal assemblies, the accent is on discussing ways to better one's performance or the performance of one's unit. In terms of the previous metaphor this kind of talk seems to be related to the way soldiers and officers tinker with the production process and with the quality of their products.

Yet for all the stress on innovation and thinking, the "brain" metaphor is subordinated to the metaphor of "machine." This is evident in the following two excerpts, the first from the exchange with Itai, the deputy battalion commander: "If you don't give the company commanders the limiting framework, and if you don't give them a degree of independence, then you lose any output you can produce from them." The second passage is from an extended talk with Ehud, commander of C company:

I don't get up in the morning and give an order here and an order there; "This is what and how I want things!" I think about things, and when I send someone I explain why it's important that he do that thing. This goes on until the stage where I say; "Okay this is after all the army. I've explained until now, and from this moment on what I say is an order."

The implication of such statements seems to be that creativity and innovation are welcome so long as they represent contributions to the greater efficiency of the military machine. Along these lines, units like this infantry battalion are populated by resourceful and reflective people who are encouraged to contribute to the innovative and multifaceted quality of their military units but within the limits imposed by the over-all machine-like "logic-of-action".[2]

War, Survival, and a Rhetoric of Emotional Control

For all of this however, my analysis does not stray far from rather conventional examinations of organizations. The combination of "machine-like" performance, bureaucratic administration, and "brain-like" innovation as guiding imagery, to put this by way of example, is not untypical of many business firms. What distinguishes military organizations are the kind of representations used in regard to the environment they are supposed to function in, are trained to perform in, namely, combat. At the risk of stating the obvious let me emphasize that the focal environment at the level of field units is combat and not war in general. What interests soldiers most of all is the localized, violent encounter of two armed organizations (Boene 1990:29). As I began to appreciate when I went over my field-notes, the portrayal of combat harbors the distinctiveness and the strength of military metaphors.

What kind of experience is combat? In the stark words of various soldiers from the battalion, combat is a matter of "survival," circumstances of "meeting danger," "the moment of truth," the "test of fear," the "critical instant," "a situation of life or death," or "a game you just can't lose." These depictions of combat are typical of any modern army where the scene of the actual fire fight is one of utmost chaos and confusion. In this situation the soldier confronts not only the imminent danger of loss of life, and perhaps more frightening the loss of limb; he also witnesses wounds and death suffered by others (Gal 1988; Moskos 1988:5). In addition, there is a constant and gnawing sense of uncertainty about the unfolding "action" on the battlefield (what has often been termed the "fog" of battle). In such a situation an overwhelming totality of sounds, smells, and sights come together in a form that individuals find very hard to analyze in any meaningful way (Shalit 1988: 147). Closely related to this experience are more "routine" stresses: the weight of the pack and the equipment, the taste and quality (or lack) of food and water, loss of sleep and at times difficult weather conditions. Keegan's (1976:47) eloquent evocation puts it thus:

> Battle, for him [the soldier], takes place in a wildly unstable physical and emotional environment; he may spend much of his time in combat as a

mildly apprehensive spectator, granted, by some freak of events, a comparatively danger-free grandstand view of others fighting; then he may suddenly be able to see nothing but the clods on which he has flung himself for safety, there to crouch – he cannot anticipate for minutes or hours; he may feel in turn, boredom, exultation, panic, anger, sorrow, bewilderment, even that sublime emotion we call courage. And his perception of community with his fellow-soldiers will fluctuate in equal measure.

In the context of the IDF one of the most common terms used to describe combat is *lachats*. The literal translation of this term into English is "pressure," but the Hebrew includes all of the synonyms and connotations of the English word: stress, anxiety, strain, or tension. What is the significance of this "pressure"? I am going to argue that it is at the juncture in which the "machine," "bureaucratic," and "brain" metaphors are applied to the highly stressful situation of combat that a whole "rhetoric of emotional control" emerges; that this emotional control under pressure – within and later outside the combat situation – comes to figure in a key schema or model of military performance; and finally, that it is this key model that is used in evaluating soldiers and actions and interpreting new situations.

Let me begin by laying bare the rhetoric of emotions that underlies talk about combat. Much of what I am going to say about emotions may appear to readers to be taken for granted, and it is so because it is "our" (i.e., Western middle-class) rhetoric. It is, of course, also this character of taken-for-grantedness that gives this theory of emotions its strength.

In our usual thinking, actions occur because of intentions. Since we do not say what is obvious, we usually do not explain action by saying it was intended (D'Andrade 1987:120). Thus in Hebrew and in English, verbs having to do with perception, thought, desire, and intention all typically predicate an active agent. In regard to feelings and emotions however, the agent is *typically* described as a passive experiencer: "Things bother, bore, or excite the subject." In general, feelings and emotions are considered to be reactions to the world that are mediated by our understanding of the world, and we often speak of them as being "triggered" by external events. Typically, then, emotions are not thought to be completely under one's control (D'Andrade 1987:119).

Closely related to these notions is the categorization of emotions by mass nouns rather than count nouns: except in poetry one does not usually say one sadness ago. Mass nouns have no defined edges that make counting possible. Furthermore, like water or color, emotions can blend so that one can experience several feelings at once. Finally, emotions are thought to cause various involuntary visceral responses such as turning pale, flushing, trembling, shedding tears, or sweating, although individual and situational responses may differ greatly. At base here is a folk theory of emotions as "things" that one (or one's group) must deal with in a functional sense (Abu-Lughod and Lutz 1990:1): the existence of these "things" – emotions and feelings created by external circumstances – creates internal states that may prove difficult to handle or regulate.

We are now in a position to return to the combat situation in which emotions, whether mass, intermingling, or externally triggered, take on prime importance for soldiers and commanders. In these circumstances, fear, apprehension, dread, and at times exhilaration blend together and issue forth within oneself *because* of the external situation. I would suggest that the problem becomes one of agency: Who will be master? Situation or person? Circumstances or (because this is such a male thing) man?

This is a problem because in combat, control of or by the situation – via emotions – is related to the overall character of the unit as a fighting machine that is acting on the environment. For example, destruction of enemy personnel and equipment or securing advantageous positions are tasks that are predicated on the management of internal feelings and emotions. Because emotions may impede the performance of military tasks they must be overcome, channeled, and above all controlled.[3] Conversely, the automaticity and the ability to react to circumstances which are required of soldiers and commanders are based on the problematic control of their internal states. This reasoning was formulated by a former brigade commander who said that the problem in combat is how a person "overcomes" (*lehitgaber*, literally "conquers" or "overpowers") the situation. In reality, one can make a further distinction that members of the unit rarely make explicit: between a more active control of emotions necessitating conscious effort, and an "automatic" curb on feelings that may arise out of training.

This point may become clearer by means of another distinction made in regard to emotions. In Lutz' (1990:70) explication, lack of control of emotions in American culture – and I would argue that by extension in most middle-class cultures in the West – is depicted as leading to uncontrolled action like "running wild" or "boiling over." The metaphor of control implies something that otherwise would be out of control, something wild and unruly, a threat to order (Lutz 1990:72). This type of argument has been propounded by Katz (1990) in her study of U.S. Army drill sergeants. She found that for these men the prime danger of emotionality is lack of control leading to uncontrolled behavior which would prove to be an obstacle to military performance.

I would argue that this is only part of the picture, for under certain situations , particularly in combat, the understood danger is not only or even primarily wild, untamed, or frenzied behavior but in a curious way its opposite: lack of action, paralysis. This aspect of uncontrolled behavior is very often implied by reference to being "pressured" in combat. The image seems to imply physical pressure on one's limbs and body that hinders intended, forceful and effective action. This image of external forces operating on all or parts of one's physical form fits "our" logic of causation: an external situation influences emotions that impede action.[4]

Talk in the IDF is replete with terms involving the relation between emotions and action. Much of this rhetoric is centered on the term "cool performance" (*kor ruach*). This phrase, which encapsulates emotional control in the service of military missions, is the one used most often in appraising performance under "pressure." The literal meaning of *kor ruach* is "cool" or "cold spirit," but it refers to the ability to act with confidence, poise, and composure under trying circumstances. Specifically, this ability involves such things as control of breath and voice while talking, giving orders smoothly, thinking clearly, reacting quickly, or even controlling one's limbs or countenance (not grimacing, for example).

A closely related term is *dvekut bamesima*, which strictly speaking means "cemented" or "glued" to one's mission but carries the connotation of carrying out one's assigned mission *despite* all of the difficulties of the combat situation. Perhaps an English equivalent of this latter term is "sticking to one's guns" during an enemy attack. Here emotional control is explicitly linked to motivation; the end result is what should be kept in sight when carrying out one's combat mission (see Schild 1973: 427). While *kor ruach* is centered on one's personal character and demeanor, *dvekut bamesima* is focused on impulsion towards the defined goals. In essence what is important both in "cool spirit" and in "cemented to one's mission" are two things: the first is the self-control needed to master a situation;[5] the second is resourcefulness in the face of disorder and impediments.

On the basis of this kind of reasoning, much of military psychotherapy is focused not only on a variety of uncontrolled behaviors but no less importantly, on the debilitating effects of combat. Indeed, shell shock or battle fatigue are expressed in terms of lack of action or as lack of control over one's body and its appendages and therefore as impediments to military performance. The very terms "combat reactions" "battle fatigue", and "functional debilitation" (Gabriel 1987: 48, 74; Shalit 1988: 103; Gal 1988) capture the notion of the soldier's involuntary response to the firefight in terms of inability to contribute to the military effort. Indeed, the clinical syndrome of battle shock includes immobility of appendages of the body, blindness and deafness without a somatic base, apathy, involuntary shuddering, and general confusion and memory loss (Levy et al. 1993).

From the perspective of my analysis, the metaphors used by American soldiers to describe their experiences of combat are illuminating in that they seem to be based on a similar rhetoric of control. Kennett (1987: 135) for instance, relates how veterans of the Second World War talk of how the blood freezes in the veins during the firefight. Similarly, the English expression "scared shitless" evokes the lack of control over one's body (and one's most intimate) activities during battles.[6]

A Key Schema: Combat

Let me relate these points back to the main line of my argument through the analysis of three short passages. The first is from the conversation with which I began this chapter. Ehud had been speaking of his experience in Lebanon:

> At that period I reached the apex of my competence in terms of activating six [mortar] barrels under conditions of pressure, night after night. Really, with successful hits, really excellent hits. And from that moment I went down in terms of my professional ability, in terms of the tension, in terms of everything.

The second passage is from an interview with Gili, an NCO; speaking of his war experiences, he said:

> I found out that the limits of my ability, and I'm not telling you anything new here, are way beyond anything I could even imagine. My ability to withstand hardships...[means] that I could meet challenges [*le-hitmoded*]... I learnt that whenever I think I've reached my limits including mental limits, I can always make an effort to continue on to act.

The third excerpt is taken from Lieblich's book (1989:128) and involves the words of a medical orderly talking of the war in Lebanon:

That's when I saw severely injured men for the first time. I reacted...outstandingly. I was cool. Professional. A leader in the situation. I acted as if I were a different person there, with a fantastic ability not to panic, to cope under stress. I think that never before or afterwards could I be that man.

Lieblich is interested, given her analytical focus, in the self-discovery of young men who underwent a kind of "peak experience" during the war. She is primarily concerned with the ways in which war and military service are a central part of becoming an adult man in Israel. Indeed, the texts from my project could be examined along similar lines. But what I would suggest is a shift of focus from the individual to the cultural level. More specifically, I argue that we may benefit by asking about the kind of cultural expectations that these peak experiences answer? Is there an underlying schema or scenario in terms of which this "peak experience" is actualized, interpreted and "made sense of"?

Let me now formulate this "folk" model— or to use interchangeable terms, key schema or prototypical scenario – of combat: Combat is a threatening situation of extreme stress and uncertainty (the chaos or "fog" of battle) in which units (combinations of soldiers, lethal equipment, and drills) under the command of officers perform their assigned tasks by mastering their emotions. The four main elements of this scenario are those we have been discussing: situation, unit, command, and emotions. The individual soldier is the juncture through which the four elements are expressed; he undertakes actions derived from membership in a machine-like organization, under extremely stressful circumstances, and masters emotions caused by the situation in order to carry out actions dictated by his commander.

Sounds simple? It is. A host of actors, equipment, organizations, and events are simplified in an expected manner for any military man. The folk model or schema of combat "works" by relating the different constituent elements together to create a more complex concept.

Now go back to the three descriptions of the "peak experience" of combat. While brief, these passages are understandable precisely because they assume a background knowledge familiar both to the speaker and to the person he interacts with. My point is simply that this knowledge is *organized* in terms of the combat schema. What people do is to match things like "activating mortars," "successful hits," or "conditions of pressure" with the main elements of the schema which is available to them as members of the culture. While the combat model is relatively uncomplicated, it is itself comprised of more complex components. (For example, the activation of mortars is itself a complicated notion of relations between men, machines, and drills.)

To restate an earlier assertion, while all of this kind of understanding is obvious and simple (to members of the culture), it is our task to explain just how this obviousness is organized and what needs the simplification serves. To put this matter figuratively, if one were to ask soldiers to put into writing the kinds of understandings basic to the three excerpts, they would fill volumes and volumes of notes and documentation. The combat schema thus allows one to encapsulate this large load of knowledge into simple and manipulable "chunks," which provide the tools for much more complex understandings and reasonings.[7] Following Hutchins (in Quinn and Holland 1987:18), I would suggest that such models or schemas serve as "templates" from which any number of propositions can be constructed (for instance, to evaluate, judge, or interpret), and it is to these matters that I turn in the next chapter.

Notes

1. Information is of vital importance in any organization, but it is crucial in military organizations, as Van Creveld (1985: 7) notes,

    > [T]he information must be gathered (about enemy, terrain, our own forces) filtered, classified, distributed, displayed... On the basis of the information thus processed an estimate of the situation must be formed. Objectives are laid down and alternative methods for attaining them worked out. A decision must be made. Detailed planning must be got under way. Orders must be drafted and transmitted, their arrival and proper understanding by the recipients verified. Execution must be monitored by means of a feedback system at which point the process repeats itself.

2. On a more micro scale, there are also limits on the innovativeness of individual soldiers, commanders, or units. As the commander of the battalion said in a briefing before a battalion exercise: "There are no arguments about techniques; there is no leeway in regard to drills."

3. A corroboration of this point is found in Katz' (1990:466) explication of how U.S. Army drill sergeants talk of feelings. According to her, these men expressed feelings in terms of body states: "My feet don't move," or "My muscles tensed and I was sweating all over." The men mentioned only those parts of the body such as muscles, eyes, bones that were directly related to action and role performances, and not the usual parts used as metaphors for emotions like the heart or digestive system.

4. I think it is no coincidence that Keegan chose to entitle his 1976 book *The Face of Battle*. The title evokes the lack of control soldiers have over their perception of combat, and the consequent need they have of dealing with the stressful situation.

5. One can find a certain analogy for this situation in the kind of poise and composure one is thought to need in such situations as mountain climbing or car racing.

6. Thus Kennett (1987: 135) cites a study of the Vietnam War that showed that about ten per cent of American soldiers reported losing control of their bowels during combat. Grossman (1995: 70) explains the physiological basis of this phenomenon: "during extremely stressful circumstances the fight-or-flight response kicks in and the sympathetic nervous system mobilizes *all* available energy for survival. In combat this often results in nonessential activities such as digestion, bladder control, and sphincter control being completely shut down. The process is so intense that soldiers very often suffer stress diarrhea, and it is not uncommon for them to urinate, defecate in their pants as the body literally "blows its ballast" in an attempt to provide all the energy resources required to ensure its survival."

7. The reasons for this kind of simplification have to do with the limits of our cognitive capacities. In technical terms the organizing principle here is one of prototype (Keesing 1987:385; Quinn 1987). These cognitive schemas tend to be composed of a small number of objects – at most seven plus or minus two – because of the constraints of short and long term memory among human beings (D'Andrade 1987:112). An example from the world of commercial exchange may clarify this point. To judge if some event is an instance of "buying," the person making the judgement must decide if there have been a seller, a buyer, merchandise, an offer and an acceptance and a transaction. The point is that since all of these criteria must be held in mind simultaneously to make this judgement with any rapidity, the criteria cannot exceed the limits of human memory. Hence, as in the "buying" model so in the combat schema the constituent elements are in themselves complex images.

INTERLUDE 4:
IN THE FIELD

The battalion's deputy commander, an engineer with an academic back-ground in physics, and I were sitting on the hood of his Jeep looking at soldiers of B company. They were going through a set of drills simulating an attack of fortified trenches on a hill nearby. Intensely curious, the officer engaged me in a conversation about the main problems or questions that underlay my research on the unit. In the rambling and rather unfocused man-ner that I sometimes use at the beginning of any stint of fieldwork, I answered that I was vaguely interested in describing the ways in which the battalion as an organization "worked." I further explained that during the early stages of any research project, I have little more than a set of rather general orienting themes. "I don't understand," he said. "What is your sample? All you've got is a population of one!" I found myself giving an impromptu talk on the benefits of case studies, qualitative approaches in the social sciences, and naturalistic methods of collecting data.

After he reflected for a few minutes, my listener commented, "I see, you seem to be furthering your career by studying us."

***

During a battalion exercise just before dawn on a moonless night, the whole unit was arrayed over a few hundred meters at the bottom of a hill we were to attack at sunrise. I walked to the side of one column, took out the little tape recorder that I used during research, and started talking into it. I

50

recorded rather mundane information about the sounds and the smells of the night and the equipment, the physical exertion, the boredom and the excitement of the maneuver. The deputy commander of the unit came up and stood quietly for a minute or two. He finally came up to me and said: "Listen, Eyal, I know that you're an anthropologist, and I know that you're strange; but have you started talking to yourself?"

4. THE MODEL IN USE: THE BATTALION AND OTHER UNITS

❧❧❧

*I*n this chapter I examine how the folk model of combat is used in the ongoing reality of the unit in order to derive the criteria by which soldiers and officers are appraised, offer prescriptions for improvement, and evaluate the value of training. I then proceed to offer a number of suggestions about the similarity between the battalion and other combat detachments of the IDF.

Evaluating Soldiers: Professionalism

The first case has to do with what are seen to be "ideal" or "good" soldiers. The following is a passage from the interview with Ehud, commander of C company. Like most of the officers in the battalion – and I suspect in the IDF as well – Ehud formulates his answer in terms of military *miktso'iyut*, or "professionalism" as in the phrase "an able soldier is a professional":

> A good soldier is one whose equipment is in order, he has his web gear in order.... He has all he needs: cartridges, canteens, water in the canteens; his specialized equipment; like if he carries a communications rig then he has all of the antennas (short and long), and that they are secured to the rig.... If he carries a light mortar then he has the proper ammo in order... Always to be meticulous about the weapons being clean, oiled... This is one side of being a professional soldier. The other side is that he be able to perform all

of the drills like the right kind of movement, quietly and with control. Also basic discipline: not to talk while on the move, not to smoke, to move quickly, not to gripe, not to be afraid of water, and not be afraid of the sun, and not to be afraid of puddles and not of dunes. All of these things make a good infantry soldier.

While this picture of an exemplary soldier may apply to any situation – small- and large-scale exercises or patrols, for example – his desired traits and qualities are derived from the basic combat schema. The criteria for judging whether a certain person deserves or does not deserve to be labeled or categorized as a "professional" are derived from the schema. The underlying systematicity of this portrayal, in other words, is based on relating the machine metaphor and the metaphor of bureaucratic discipline to the metaphor of emotional control, and through these to military actions.

The next two excerpts concern not "ideal" soldiers but real situations. The first example is from a slightly bemused report a medical orderly gave me of his conduct during one training exercise in the desert:

> We were in the midst of a long set of maneuvers, and one of the company's soldiers lost lots of liquids. I had to give him an infusion there in the field, and from that day on I had a name of someone who knows how to stick in an infusion.... Any medic could have done that, but it does show a minimum of professional ability to function under those kinds of conditions.

The next passage is a characterization of a soldier that Omer, commander of the support company, had under his command during the Intifada:

> He is a constant talker; he jabbers away incessantly (*kashkeshan peraee*). But the reasons for throwing him out [of the unit] were not related to that but to his being irresponsible. He's the type where you can't anticipate his reactions: you go to a village and he suddenly begins to run after someone, and he'll disappear into some alley and he won't even think about the fact that he's endangering himself and that everyone has to look for him. Simply irresponsible... So I decided to get rid of him. He is excitable, has a higher level of excitability than others.

In both passages the link between responsibility, reliability and self-control is most explicit. In these cases concepts derived from the basic scenario, such as performance, emotional control, and endangering situation, are used to evaluate soldiers in threatening situations. In the first instance this assessment is related to the medic's performance under stressful conditions in the field. In the second, the appraisal is carried out by pointing to how the schema or scenario of "proper" action has been disrupted. Both cases, then, exemplify how the set of conditions and behavior posited in the prototypical scenario form a basis for evaluation of concrete instances.

The scenario can also be used in self-evaluation. The following words are from an interview with an ex-fighter. After many years of service in the support company he had become a driver and was explaining the advantages he brought with him to his new role:

> I'm just trying to think of an engagement (*hitaklut*). In terms of my past, I was in three wars and I hope I haven't changed in terms of my ability not to run away. I don't really know. You would have to try me again now, but I begin from the assumption that a driver who has worked in a canteen all of his life and never experienced pressure, never had a tough experience like being under fire, will behave differently in a critical situation. Here [patrolling Israel's northern borders] the minute we find ourselves in an engagement I find myself a fighting soldier [*lochem*, literally "warrior"] and I have to man the machine gun.

To make the reasoning here explicit, through contrasting himself to other soldiers who have not been in battle, the driver's self-evaluation is also an assertion of his greater military importance. Here again, combat is the test, *the* set of criteria for the measure of true soldiership.

Prescriptions for proper military behavior are based on a similar reasoning which links self-control and performance. For instance, soldiers are constantly being exhorted to restrain their use of ammunition during exercises, or not to go wild with their guns (*lo lehishtolel*) during combat patrols, the Intifada, maneuvers, or proof firing. Dan, commander of B company, talks to his troops before an armed patrol along the border with Lebanon: "We've been here many days and have only three more to go. We will restrain ourselves, we will curb ourselves."

Again, in one session devoted to summing up a battalion exercise, the brigade commander, an officer belonging to the permanent force, commented about the machine gunners' performance:

> You carried out your missions well, but, pardon the words, every once in a while you seemed to be reaching an orgasm while firing. You neglected to take into account the situation, like the fact that if this were a real battle you

would be exposing yourself to enemy fire. Don't take leave of your senses because you can get killed.

Emotional control is thus figuratively linked to survival and to effectiveness. Perhaps an English equivalent of this notion is the danger of becoming "trigger happy", that is, letting the exhilaration of firing lead to uncontrolled use of weapons. Similarly, the same battalion commander constantly encouraged company and platoon commanders "not to take pity on the men and on themselves" during drills, and not to "yield" or "surrender" (*levater*) to the men during maneuvers despite their fatigue, hunger or thirst.

Trust and Survival: Evaluating Commanders

The key scenario depicts different (albeit overlapping and complementary) roles for soldiers and for commanders (primarily but not only officers). As in other armies (Boene 1990: 31), a minimum amount of courage is expected of the rank and file combatant, as well as a capacity to control fear in face of danger, discomfort, pain, or misfortune. Of the leader, however, much more is expected: more composure, additional competence, greater self-control, and an ability to lead by inspiration and by example.

This kind of reasoning is applied in the following passage in which Eran, deputy commander of the support company, appraises a platoon commander in his company:

> He is an officer, he has emotional maturity, and he knows how to lead people, how to give orders. He knows to distinguish between what is important and unimportant.... He isn't a little boy who will cry every time he has to go out on patrol like some of these other guys we have in the battalion.

Notice two points in regard to this passage. First, the use of children as the contrastive category of people one should not behave like. Along these lines, in a variety of situations soldiers are exhorted "not to act spoilt," and "not to behave like babies," or are advised before patrol that "summer camp is over; now is the army." Only rarely, and in contrast to the U.S. Marines, for example is the contrastive category that of women (Eisenhart 1975; Cameron 1994). Categorizing someone as a child in the circumstances of the unit allows the categorizer both to point to a desired set of behaviors and to negatively label the person being categorized.[1] The second point is that implicit in this commander's words is not only an elevation of his ability to control his emotions like an adult (like the self-evaluation of the driver that I brought in earlier). It is also an implicit plea for the legitimacy of his position as a *commander* directing others. It is an implicit argument for his right to exercise power within the military hierarchy *because* of his personal qualities.

In their evaluation of commanders, soldiers use two similar criteria derived from the combat schema: professionalism (the machine and brain metaphors) and emotional control. Thus, for example, a young NCO told me that in general "officers tend to control themselves much more [than soldiers]". The following rather typical example from an interview with Noam, a veteran NCO now a clerk, is similar in tone. We were speaking about the "ideal" officer and he said:

> Yes ,well, it's his professionalism (*miktsoi'yut*); like how he moves the forces, how he navigates. If it's a commander who can't find his way then you don't like being with him. I mean that in the end if your commander, and especially the company commander, is not professional, then your feeling is not good, insecure; because you know that you may have to go out with him to war one day, a very bad feeling. We had one platoon commander like that with us in Lebanon. He was a nice guy but not very good professionally and in the end he was thrown out... I wouldn't go with someone like that to war, I wouldn't be calm [*lev shaket*, literally, "with a calm heart"] like I was with Omri or Nimrod [two former battalion commanders], people that you feel are professional and know how to manage, and know how to give clear orders, and who will get you out of there alive.

A commander's ability to impart or inspire a feeling of security among his troops is a theme that came up time and again in the interviews. In this respect, officers must grapple with two kinds of emotional control: their own, and those of the soldiers under their command. Indeed, officers more than other soldiers are typically thought of as directly influencing soldiers' abilities to control their emotions. For example, many soldiers spoke of the feeling of security they got when their commanders gave orders in a smooth way, without mistakes or hesitation. In their eyes, an officer's cool performance in itself helped them in the tense situation. Accordingly, in a conversation we were having over coffee one day, a machine gunner noted:

> Do you remember Eran? He is cool (*kar*) and gives his troops a feeling of security. This is especially important when you're under pressure. During

these periods it's especially important that someone give you confidence (*bitachon*, also security), calm you and direct you. Do you remember how Eran was in the ambush we laid. He waited until the terrorists were only a few meters from us before opening fire.

Again Ehud (commander of C Company), a few days after our initial conversation said to me that he had been mulling over one of my questions and that the important thing for a commander is "to instill (*lintoa*, literally "implant") a feeling of security among his soldiers."

The criteria used to appraise officers are not only applied to firefights. They are often employed in regard to more mundane situations. One company commander, in talking of the atmosphere his predecessor had created, used standards drawn from the combat model in order to underscore the predecessor's lack of success:

> All those time-timetables [deadlines] that he set for the men. He didn't allow them enough vacations to go home. He applied pressure all of the time as though there was a war going on.... Too much pressure! He and the [platoon] commanders sort of went wild (*mishtolelanim*).

A few moments later in the interview he talked about a fellow officer in his company and invoked the image of controlled use of weapons: "Well, he tends to shoot from the hip when he's making decisions, while I tend to think before deciding, I shoot through the rearsights."

Officers are clearly aware of the criteria soldiers use in appraising their performance as commanders. Consequently they often consciously and intentionally present a certain military "self" to their subordinates. Officers told me that they often felt that in stressful situations there arose a need to give the impression, through various "techniques", of being in control. Basic to their reasoning was the assumption that by setting an example of emotional control they would infuse their troops with a greater measure of certainty and security and therefore influence their emotions. Thus in speaking about his commanding officer, a medical orderly told me that "the minute the doctor becomes pressured, the medical orderly does not function."

The following passage is from a discussion with a former company commander:

> The professionalism of the company commander is very important for soldiers. They can tell you that you're a son of a bitch but if you're professional then it's okay.... It has a lot to do with [interpersonal] politics: how he [the

company commander] presents himself and what he does. Like whether he's insecure or he shows that he is in charge is all a matter of politics, a sort of constant example for the men. If he shows that he's in charge in a forceful and controlled way, the soldiers begin to accept all he says.

Another officer once observed that he was rather proud of himself and his self-control despite the fact that he was never really calm about matters (*af pa'am lo shaket*):

> I never get angry, do I? I try not to get emotional and to give orders in a clear way.... Take the way to speak on the communications net: think before you talk. Don't start yapping away and get suddenly stuck. Think and then give orders shortly and curtly.

Given the various criteria derived from the combat schema, it may now be clearer how new members of the unit are appraised. Gathering a large amount of information on each new arrival is unnecessary (Holland and Skinner 1987:105). All one need do is to check for a number of characteristics in terms of the *potential* performance of the new member under conditions of battle. Thus for example, all one has to say of a new officer is that he is someone who is liable to be pressured easily (*lachtsan*), for a whole set of connotations rooted in the scenario of combat to be understood. Along these lines, when looking at a new platoon commander briefing his troops, commanding them in an exercise, or simply making sure that they are on time for some activity, the company or battalion commanders may be running a sort of mental simulation model of how the new officer would behave under combat conditions. A few rather simple clues from his ongoing behavior are used as a basis for judgement.

The advantages of the cultural model lie in its facilitation of communication; experiences, appraisals, or prescriptions can be rapidly communicated to other people *because* they are formulated according to shared conventions. Thus a few words exchanged during a meeting are usually enough to portray a situation or a person. The price of this cognitive economy, however, is some rigidity in interpreting the world and a certain slowness in recognizing or learning new models (Holland and Skinner 1987:105). In the context of my case, while the shared schema of soldiering allows one to discuss and communicate about a highly complex world in manageable terms, the schema may restrict the understanding and the ability to react to novel situations.

Training: Simulation of the Prototypical Scenario

Most soldiers, including those of the Israeli army, devote much more time to training than to participation in any sort of warfare. Given the centrality of war preparation, it is not surprising that training activities, whether focused on individual skills or involving group exercises, are derived from, and involve simulations of, the prototypical scenario of combat. From an organizational point of view, training (drills and maneuvers) are devised with two interrelated purposes in mind: to enhance the "combat readiness" of units (Shafritz et al. 1989:290), and as fabricated tests in lieu of the ultimate test of combat. A number of points follow from this understanding.

In the battalion, as in any fighting unit, many drills are related to weapons and weaponry. Repetitive training is designed to produce a conditioned reflex in weapons handling (field-stripping, aiming, or handling technical stoppages). Many scholars have noted the strong stress on automaticity found in military training. Holmes (1986:42), for instance, observes that within the stress of the firefight, "drills help minimize the randomness of battle, and give the soldier familiar points of contact in an uncertain environment, like lighthouses in a stormy sea." Keegan (1976:70) also notes that given the essentially chaotic nature of combat, the conduct of war has been reduced to a set of rules and a system of procedures in military education.

But Shalit's observations suggest that there is another element involved here. He states that as "one becomes accustomed to certain conditions (for example, handling explosives), one considers them less risky" (Shalit 1988: 114). What he seems to be talking about is that weapons training pertains to the inculcation of certain emotional attitudes *toward* weapons. It is through the use of military instruments that troops carry out missions, but these implements are in themselves dangerous. In a curious way, weapons become mediators between the soldier and his environment. On the one hand, they are a "continuation" of his body and an essential part of the man-drill-equipment complex. Yet on the other hand, weapons are "extensions" of the dangerous environment because of their lethality. Thus the problem becomes one of learning to feel secure with, and in charge of, the lethal instruments one operates.

Along these lines, much talk in the battalion is devoted to such things as the need to "master" (*lishlot*, literally "control") guns and firearms. This mastery, I was told, is achieved through repeated practice and the firing of live ammunition, both of which lead to a situation in which the men become less afraid of such implements. According to a number of officers and NCOs the aim of these practices is to inculcate a sense of *bitachon baneshek*, or what can be roughly translated as a combination of "trust" and "confidence" in (one's) weapon.[2] This term evokes the sentiment of a safe, confident use of a lethal implement without anxiety or apprehension, and a belief that the implement will work according to one's expectations. The point here (although it is not one that was elucidated explicitly in the battalion) is that the infantry soldier may have a special connection to combat. It well may be, then, that just as his relationship to his weapon is perceived to be much more personal than the link between a tank or artillery crew and the weapons they operate, so his relation to the circumstances of battle is less mediated than for the soldiers of other ground forces.

The appraisal of many drills designed to implant "confidence in weapons" should be seen in this light. These exercises include shooting in firing ranges (before and after physical exertion), weapons tests at the beginning of training drills or before embarking on combat patrols, and participating in diverse live-fire exercises (from the squad to the brigade levels). Frequently, various kinds of meetings and gatherings are held after or during such activities, and matters related to weaponry become objects for deliberation and discussion. Just like sports coaches working with athletes on improving performance through "mental" preparation, so commanders and peers use such opportunities to comment and elaborate on ways to upgrade their soldiers' performance with guns.

More generally, training exercises in which the whole battalion or its constituent parts (companies and platoons) participate become tests in which many of the criteria derived from the combat schema come into play: composure under pressure, the machinelike operation of units and sub-units, or the ability to react to, and innovate in, a changing environment. In this respect, while the men are fully aware of the differences between real and simulated combat, exercises are more than rehearsals. Because maneuvers are carried out with live ammunition, mock (and at times real) casualties, irregular food and drink, and conditions of fatigue and uncertainty, these events are taken to be "serious" in ways that rehearsals are not. Along these lines, the set of criteria officers and soldiers use most often in appraising these events is their similarity to real combat: the types and amounts of weapons used, their duration, the physical difficulties involved, or the complexity and uncertainty on which they are based (see also Gal 1986:149).

For example, soldiers and officers link the seriousness, prestige, and attraction of an exercise with the kinds of weapons and ammunition employed. The men differentiate between "wet runs" (*targilim retuvim*) that are maneuvers carried out with live ammunition and "dry runs" (*targilim yeveshim*) which are practice sessions executed without such munitions. While the first type is considered dangerous, risky, and therefore interesting and challenging, the second is considered to be boring and "colorless".[3] Even if no real ammunition is involved, an exercise or training drill can be more engrossing if at least imitation ammunition (bullets, grenades, and charges) that make noise and smoke is used. Soldiers and officers also discriminate between the diverse kinds of weapons wielded; for example, if an exercise involves tanks, antitank missiles, or artillery, then it is considered more life-like and therefore more serious, engaging, and impressive.

The men often explicitly linked the type of ammunition used to the strength of their motivation for participating in training. At the end of one training stint, an NCO told me that after a week of little or no sleep and general fatigue, everyone in his company nevertheless seemed to wake up for the final battalion exercise, which involved air support, artillery, and tanks. In a similar vein, the battalions's deputy commander said that a "real" exercise generates a great deal of excitement and tension in the troops, who suddenly seem to find new strength and to enjoy their performance and the performance of the unit as a whole. Soldiers often stated that these large-scale exercises are opportunities for them to express their professionalism, and that they often take on as much live ammunition as they or their machines (usually APCs) can carry.

My fieldnotes are full of references to such thinking. For example, when I visited a rifle company prior to a company exercise, some of the soldiers discussed their universal preference for using at least simulation grenades and bullets rather than carry out just another "boring exercise without live fire." In a similar vein, one young radio man who had joined the battalion a year before the exercise complained that all he did was carry the communications device and did not get the reward of firing his gun: "It's just not worth it [participating in the exercise], my efforts." A platoon sergeant reported that after a week of having no more than two or three hours of sleep, the men began the concluding battalion exercise feeling very tired. Yet although the final exercise involved walking about 20 kilometers, when the shooting began everyone started to "fly" (*la-toos*). When we talked about live-fire field exercises the deputy CO of the battalion said:

A good exercise injects a lot of tension into the matter; every one becomes more energetic (*nimratzim*), has more strength. This is also a good opportunity to show one's professional competence (*meyumanut miktso'it*). Take a look at how the machine gunners never grumble or complain. The ones that complain are the riflemen. More than that, everyone tends to lug more weight and ammunition before a live exercise than at other times. Sometimes the soldiers even steal ammunition from each other.

When discussing the fact that almost all soldiers and officers of the unit like to fire their guns, a young platoon commander thought for a while and then observed that, "part of the element in firing involves the knowledge that the thing in your hand kills and the power you have in your hands. This pumps up the adrenalin like in sports".

Officers, however, often evaluate exercises according to criteria derived from the brain metaphor. For example, Ari, the current battalion commander, was slightly vexed with me when I suggested that the unplanned part of the battalion exercise (that is, the part where the reactive capacities of commanders are most fully tested) may be superfluous. "Are you kidding" he protested, "this is exactly the most interesting part of the whole maneuver".

Within the Unit: Sharedness and Typicality

Before moving on to deal with images of the enemy, it may be opportune to deal with a few comparative issues. Two questions suggest themselves in this regard: the distribution of cultural knowledge within the battalion, or the degree to which the schema characterize different kinds of soldiers and officers; and, the existence of this model in other units of the Israeli armed forces, or the extent to which my unit is typical of the IDF.

First, in terms of the distribution of knowledge across organizational positions within the unit, I made a conscious effort to gather information not only from officers but also from NCOs, "'ordinary'" soldiers, and from administrative and technical personnel. When I began to analyze my material I expected to find great differences between the views of combat troops and soldiers in administrative capacities. I anticipated that because these two groups of people were called upon to carry out different tasks they would be appraised (and appraise themselves) on the basis of different models of (military) action. What I found, however, was a very wide consensus among all members of the battalion showing what appears to be a similar kind of cognitive organization of knowledge among almost all of the unit's soldiers. In addition, while officers could, on the whole, formulate the general contours of the model in a comprehensive way, almost all "ordinary" soldiers also used them to describe and evaluate military service, missions, and the quality of their units.

The reasons for this relative homogeneity have to do with the processes of selection and socialization that troops in such units undergo. First, soldiers in the battalion have all undergone a double "sieve" of selection: during the compulsory term of service and again during reserve duty. In each stage, soldiers who do not "fit" the governing organizational climate are selected out (and assigned to other units). Second, the troops who remain in combat units are socialized to operate in close, relatively cohesive companies where the small group dynamics with equals and relations with commanders reinforce the governing modes of thinking. Third, as many of the administrative staff of the unit are ex-combat soldiers, the resemblance in attitudes cuts across specific roles. All in all, like the troops of other combat battalions, and unlike the unit of combat engineers portrayed in Feige and Ben-Ari (1991), the soldiers of the battalion are a rather homogenous bunch. This assertion does not imply that there are not individual differences between men, but rather underscores the widespread acceptance of the cognitive model I have been analyzing.

A good example can be drawn from the words of the previous Brigade Commander who had over twenty-five years of experience with infantry units in the IDF and a two-year experience commanding our brigade. His thoughts encapsulate the main elements of the combat schema and also suggest how widely this model is accepted:

> The minute you pass the stage of fear, you can bring all that you have to bear on the situation... It's not that there's no one that is not frightened. You have to be an idiot not to be afraid. There are those extreme cases of people who cannot conquer their fear, but most of the people that we are talking about, soldiers, commanders and so on, they are frightened.
>
> What happens to them is that they overcome their fear; and fear is something that accompanies you all of the time. Listen, you can be walking and suddenly someone can shoot at you. What do you expect? You expect us not to be frightened? You have to be an idiot not to be frightened; there's something wrong with you if you're not afraid. That's why I said that the problem is the crisis of overcoming fear....
>
> Now, the advantage of reserve units is that almost all of the men, in one way or another, have gone through a "test of fear." Here and there, in skirmishes, deployment etc.

While his reflections were prompted by a question about the battalion in which I served, perhaps a more interesting question pertains to the wider representativeness of this unit.

Other Units

To what extent is the battalion typical of other combat units in the IDF? To what extent is the combat model characteristic of the IDF in general, or of specific parts of it? My answer to these questions is that while the greatest similarity is found among infantry units, a general resemblance is also found between such detachments and other elements of the Israeli military's field forces, primarily the armored corps. At the same time, however, I should explain that I have not carried out any piece of comparative research on other units of the IDF. Rather, my assertions are based on the findings of other scholars, the impressions of military professionals, and some reports found in Hebrew newspapers.

Let me begin with a few examples taken from another research project on other infantry units. A fascinating paper written by a student at the Hebrew University attempted to examine the reasoning of infantry soldiers and officers in regard to engagements with Palestinian fighters in Lebanon.[4] The student interviewed soldiers who had either served during Israel's invasion of Lebanon or participated in military missions in the southern part of that country. Oren, a platoon commander in the paratroopers, participated in three skirmishes during the Lebanon war:

> During the first time there was a feeling between dread and tautness for combat for the "real thing." But the minute it happens, you become an automaton [*automat*], and it expresses itself in the cancellation of emotions.... During the skirmish you are a soldier and that's it. It's amazing.... There's nothing emotional about the situation. You shoot, even without thinking about self-defense. It is a natural mechanism that works like an electrical switch.... During the activity [skirmish] one of my soldiers got killed. I looked at him and continued to attack. It didn't do anything to me – no emotional reaction. I acted properly and continued to shoot. On the one hand, it's completely irrational; and on the other hand, it's absolutely rational....
>
> I remember when I was a soldier [before becoming an officer], and that my commander was really a figure that influenced me in getting up for the assault. I would call it emotional calmness (*sheket nafshi*, literally "quiet spirit") in combat. As a soldier I knew that I could attack undisturbed and

that my platoon commander will worry about the battle; he'll know what to do at any moment....

Notice how the manner in which this man talks of his experiences corresponds very strongly with the main elements of the combat schema. First, he uses the language of machinery (automaton, mechanism, electric switch). Second, he focuses on emotional control (emotional distancing, no reflection about himself, calmness). Third, he links both elements to his performance as a soldier and to the missions of his unit (assaulting, shooting, attacking). Fourth, he links his actions to the emotional security granted by his commander.

The words of Tomer, also a paratrooper, echo those of Oren:

> I remember that there was a command of "get ready to assault". I waited and then heard the next command and that was it; I didn't think, didn't deliberate. The head was like empty; there was only an expectation and uncertainty.... Listen, you simply work like a machine, like a robot.

By using a picture of "the head" being empty, this soldier expresses the emotional distance necessitated by combat; he even distanced his "mind" from himself.

Uriel, an ex-deputy company commander in the Givati Brigade, had to take over from his superior during an engagement when the latter was wounded:

> As commander of the force I had to organize everything, and within the engagement itself I had to make sure all of the time that the force will "create fire" [constantly shoot], throw grenades, and so on. I remember that in the second before the assault I was really scared because the bullets were in our hair, but I thought that "we have to solve this problem" and I got up....

Being a commander, Uriel explicated principles related to the brain metaphor (organizing, solving problems) very explicitly. Moreover, he directly linked these principles, via emotional control, to the achievement of the tasks assigned to his force (within the threatening situation of combat).

The similarity between my battalion and other infantry units is not surprising, and there are a number of social and organizational conditions which give rise to this resemblance in attitudes and outlooks. Soldiers enter reserve units after having served in one of the IDF's infantry brigades. Moreover, throughout their military careers, they come into constant contact with men of other infantry units, be they of the reserves or the permanent military forces. This contact takes place during professional instruction (in various frameworks such as basic training, NCO courses, or officer courses), training (maneuvers and exercises on a variety of levels) and operational deployment (in an assortment of settings). But what of other field units?

The contrast raised time and again in academic, professional, military, and popular thought is the one between the infantry and the armored corps. The words of Ari, the ex-battalion commander, are instructive in this respect. His words reveal wider understandings or assumptions about the special kind of professionalism that is said to be needed by infantry soldiers. During his interview, I asked him about the distinctiveness of "infantry work". He replied;

> The life of the armored person is much simpler. His training is much more established (*kevu'im*, literally "fixed") in different matters like formations or drills.... Of course there are difficult physical sides to his work, but he doesn't have to know how to fight in a built-up area, in an open area, and how to move across obstacles; doesn't have the physical marches and the professionalism of operating different kinds of weapons let alone handling helicopters, and parachuting and joint exercises. You understand, he is a driver of a tank.... In contrast to us for example, at night they are in the tank, stuck together without anything to do. We need to learn to be quiet at night, and it becomes intimate when you talk to someone.

Indeed, this kind of wisdom reflects wider perceptions of the unique qualities and culture of infantry and armored units. Ben Shalit (1988: 121) was a military psychologist in the IDF. His observations regarding the paratroopers reveal a very common notion held by soldiers and officers (and scholars) about the infantry. To reiterate a point I made in an earlier chapter, readers would do well to remember that it is ideas and mental models that I am discussing here (and not necessarily differences in behavior or action):

> The operational mode of the paratroops is based on small units with a high degree of flexibility and autonomy. Each individual is directly involved in action and can personally affect the results of the troop's actions. He often has to make independent decisions; and although the general plans are laid out, he has to adapt and extemporize a great deal in varying conditions, and to show a great deal of initiative. In contrast, a tank crew has a much more rigid framework in which to cooperate. The technical and mechanical para-

meters are critical limiting factors affecting all members of the crew as a unit. Exact routines and rigid procedures are required. Each member of the crew has restricted and predetermined functions, which must be rigidly followed so that the unit may function as a whole. Their freedom of individual choice, as well as their chance of individual initiative, is very limited, compared with that of that paratrooper or even an ordinary infantry soldier.

A booklet that is disseminated throughout the Israeli military echoes many of these themes. The small handbook, based on research carried out by two social psychologists, is devoted to an examination of what soldiers and officers see as the chief characteristics of excellent or outstanding platoon commanders in the IDF's field units (infantry, armor, artillery and combat engineering) (Landau and Zakai 1994). The authors conclude with the following points:

> [A]mong all of the platoon commanders the focus of excellence is on the image of "the professional" attributed to them. At the same time, while in the infantry units the image of professional is a general one and usually refers to someone who "knows what to do" and is expert in all spheres: in the armored units, professionalism is more specific and is linked to knowledge of tank warfare and familiarity with drills.... In the infantry units the setting of high expectations [by platoon commanders] is expressed in a general expectation that the soldier will invest and extract the maximum of his personal potential, while in the armored and artillery units the high expectations are expressed primarily in demands to meet [technical] standards, precision regarding details, and a demand for discipline in all areas.

These differences seem to echo (and correspond to) the historical distinction between the pre-state Palmach and the British Army. Ronen (1993), links these two pre-state traditions of leadership and military organization with two traditions instituted after the establishment of the state: that of the paratroopers (or more generally, the infantry) and that of the armored corps. He concludes that the differences are between organizations that tend to emphasize order, discipline, and management and those that stress initiative, surprise, and attack. But Ronen goes on to note that underlying seeming disparities in outlook is a complex resemblance. He focuses on leadership styles and notes:

> [T]his is a conflict between two basic conceptions of leadership: the one, voluntary leadership, is informal, based on personal courage, and suitable for a small and qualitative army; the second is formalist, disciplined, professional,

and effective in large frameworks.... But in combination they are part of the *singular* image of the leader in the IDF (Ronen 1993: 128, emphasis added).

Hence, in contradistinction to Shalit I would argue that in reality, different IDF units (infantry and armor) are characterized less by a blunt contrast of orientations than by distinct mixes, different emphases, in outlook (see also Goldberg-Weil 1996). To be sure, there are variations between units. It is also true, however, that in reality infantry troops must master a great number of fixed drills, and that in action armored units need initiative and autonomy. It is in this light that van Creveld's conclusions about the general standards of the IDF should be understood:

> [I]ndividual daring (*heaza*), maintenance of aim (*dvekut bamatara*), improvisation (*iltur*), and resourcefulness (*tushia*), all... still remain key elements of the fighting doctrine that the IDF systematically inculcates into, and demands of, troops and commanders at every level (1985: 196).

Again, in a volume devoted to the armies of the Middle East we find the following assessment of the IDF: "Efficiency, initiative, improvisation, inventiveness and originality are more prized than discipline, family background, or military formality" (Levin and Halevy 1983: 7). Moreover, commentators like Van Creveld or Levin and Halevy are not alone among scholars who have noted the significant homogeneity of outlook – or ethos – of the IDF (see Schild 1973; Schiff 1995).

Why is this so? Three interrelated answers suggest themselves. First, since infantry training is a basic component of many military courses (especially commanders' courses), soldiers are exposed to criteria drawn from the combat schema throughout their periods of service (Goldberg-Weil 1996). Second, because most senior officers and virtually all of the recent commanders-in-chief of the IDF have come from the ranks of the infantry, a uniform approach is rather systematically disseminated throughout the army's field detachments. And third, as almost all of the IDF's combat units carry out infantry missions during at least part of their operational deployment, the performance of soldiers continues to be appraised according to the same criteria.

Haim Laskov, one of the Israeli army's first chiefs-of-staff, and one who contributed greatly to the IDF's initial design, sets out his views in a preface to John Ellis' *The Sharp End of War* (1980) that was translated into Hebrew under the auspices of the Ministry of Defence. Because Laskov is well-known for his disciplined professionalism and for instilling the values of the British army in Israel, it is fascinating to note how his words echo the many elements of the model of combat. He begins his preface by observing that the book paints an image of the soldier of the modern battleground:

> He looks around him clearly, simply, without an emotional load, under the frightful conditions of war; and it becomes a tactical necessity to instill in the soldier steadfast courage, that will dictate to him to move forward by disregarding fear, to attack, and in this way to master a situation of need, fatigue, and threat and danger; and all of this during a time when the logic of survival declares that the rational thing to do is to run away or hide....
>
> One of the thoughts that this book raises is that... although tomorrow comes after today, it does not mean that it is a continuation of today; It is not just a matter of pulling out a ready-made plan that has been prepared for each specific situation (Laskov 1980: 10–11; author's translation).

Laskov's terms, once more, all revolve around themes of mastering the threatening environment of combat, striving to achieve military missions, and grappling with constantly changing circumstances. Laskov's piece, however, is interesting not only because it reflects a widely accepted way of thinking in the Israeli armed forces. No less importantly, his preamble should be seen as an example of a genre of military writing that is very popular in contemporary Israel. Various publications – books, handbooks, brochures, pamphlets – some published through formal military institutions and some outside of them, serve to constantly disseminate and propagate the main tenets of the IDF's military culture. (See for example Bar-Kochva 1989; Eitan 1985; Eldar 1993; Kahalani 1988; Lev 1984; Rosenthal 1989.)

Yet Laskov's preface does not introduce a book written about the Israeli army, but rather about the military establishment of another country. Hence, let me offer a final comment about the similarity in thinking between the IDF and other armies. What I have found are reflections, impressions and insights rather than systematic scholarly comparisons, but they tend to show that, despite some differences, the similarity between the IDF and the armed forces of other industrialized democracies is quite strong. This resemblance is related not only to the use of imagery derived from industrial machinery or factory production in evaluations of, and prescriptions for, soldiers and military "work" (see Shay 1995: 205). Rather, the similarity extends to the basic model of combat. While the following passage is not a verbatim report of actual conversations, it does give one a sense of the basic resemblance across national contexts. Summarizing her research among veterans of the Vietnam War, Greenhouse observes:

> These soldiers.... fought as the artists of war they had been trained to be. The veterans' accounts to me were of the discipline of war: the ability to bear danger, to shoot without being able to see one's target, to be able to repair any machine without adequate tools, to be able to master fear and grief and revulsion. War demands perfection, and war is a mighty judge, since mistakes cost lives (1989:56).

Here again, making sense of this passage entails using the main elements of the combat schema: for example, mastering emotions, performance of tasks, an enterprising spirit, and the perils of battle. Similar understandings underlie portraits of troops during the Second World War. These were "soldiers who could control their fear, think with some clarity, and use initiative in situations where they were not under direct supervision – and to do all of these things along with considerable physical exertion" (Kennett 1987: 136).

The source of the similarity between the IDF and other military establishments is related to the soldierly role: specifically, to the kinds of missions (and environments within which) troops are asked to perform. Because of the centrality of violence to this role and the characteristic threats of battle, soldiers the world over must be socialized into a role that has rigid parameters for control of individual expressions of aggression and coercion (Katz 1990: 459). My point is thus that as organizations charged with the management of violence, IDF units partake of certain characteristics – what may be termed the 'logic of combat' – that are similar the world over, at least during our historical period. Another source of affinity is related to the historical development of military organizations (Dandeker 1992): specifically, to the evolution of combat in modern, i.e., mechanized and industrialized, armies.

While there is a very basic similarity between such armies in terms of the combat schema, in the following two chapters I analyze some differences. In Chapter 6 I deal with a few issues related to how IDF and American troops view enemies. In Chapter 7 I consider some variations in terms of models of cohesion.

NOTES

1. This does not mean that there is no place for childlike behaviors to be expressed. One medic told me that because of the overall pressure of military service he often feels the need for some self-indulgence like buying many chocolates.

2. As Shalit more generally notes, a "well-drilled routine of acting in a specific situation is of great benefit… [and contributes] to confidence in the weapon and in the military in general" (1988: 140).
3. Thus by extension, one can say, as one company commander did during operational deployment, that things are "dry," to mean boring, lacking all interest.
4. Thanks to Oz Shimon for use of his data.

INTERLUDE 5:
SOLDIERING THE INTIFADA

The following are excerpts from an interview I held with the commander of the support company a few months after the battalion's first deployment in the Intifada in the city of Hebron. He had been the commander of this company for the previous two years. As he was studying economics at the Hebrew University, we sat in my office at an establishment named (of all things) The Harry S. Truman Research Institute for the Advancement of Peace.

I remember that the first time we went to the Intifada it was six or seven months after it began. It looked very violent, very difficult. That's what they showed on television. And I expected it to be very difficult; that is, I expected that we were going to war. It was not a routine matter. I came with a lot of apprehension, and I couldn't imagine how we would grapple with this thing with all that we saw in the media. And after a week, I think, we settled into the routine there. Within a week you already understand what's going on.... It's not very pleasant, and it's not a routine kind of work there like we usually do, but you learn how to settle in. Many times it appears to be like a sort of game; it's a game how to grapple with it. There is a certain problem and you have to come up with the solution. You separate yourself from all sorts of thoughts like what am I doing here, and how and why things are happening here....

Q: *When you say a problem, you mean like a crossword puzzle?*
A: *It's a matter of technique, of how you deal with the situation. We were lucky in general because we knew the area and they prepared for us all sorts of problems, especially in the area of the kasbah [the Palestinian market] with all the alleys. It's a very dense area, and they come to throw rocks at you from the top of the*

buildings; and it's a problem because they know the area very well and they have lookouts. And at the beginning they make fun of you, but then you learn: you learn to analyze the area and to find the right techniques like patrols or where to find them or who to send there in order to deal with the situation. I think that many of the locals treated it, from what I saw, also as a game; they treated it like a game until something happened, like until one of their guys got hit. The truth is that I think that it's like a mechanism to treat it as a game. It disconnects you from all sorts of thoughts about what you are doing there....

Q: *Did these issues ever arise?*
A: *On a general level, there is the level of politics of what we are doing there, of dealing with civilians. And I wanted to disengage the company from these things. I didn't always succeed, but I wanted to, because I felt that it would be in the way of them carrying out what they had to do. For example, if you're "anti" the whole thing, let's say you're aware of doing things you should not be doing. You can't solve all sorts of technical problems if you discuss the whole idea of it all of the time.*

Q: *When did you use violent means?*
A: *That time we went into the villages. We thought we were going on a picnic. I talked to the brigade commander and he told me that things were quiet there. So we went with three vehicles and we prepared sandwiches and it was Saturday afternoon [the day of rest among Jews] and we thought that we were out for a trip. But when we arrived at the first village we saw that it was all different. You see a roadblock and then another roadblock and then another and another in the whole village. And I decided that we would clear everything up. And when we crossed the first roadblock we saw them massing, hundreds of them on both sides of the valley. We got off the vehicles and spread out with proper spacing and we began to walk. And then they began to throw stones at us. At the beginning it's frightening, but you get used to it because you see where the rocks are coming from. But when we entered the village they started to come from the rooftops and from every dominating ground. And we saw that they were quite tough, and that they fight, and that they don't run away quickly. They work with very good techniques, and they catch you at your weakest points.*

So I sent some men to hold the dominating positions and we ourselves massed and started to yell and run after them. And the minute they saw us doing this they began to run. But they would only run so far so that we wouldn't get them. And then in the middle of the village they massed again, and in order to scatter them we used the gas. We threw gas at them. And then we ran after them again.

It worked well. And from that point of view, our work in the situation was good. From my point of view as commander of the company the men operated under a stressful situation that is not easy, in a good way. And I think that the locals were also impressed and they also began pretty quickly to move back.

73

***

*During parts of my service in Hebron I observed many things (as adminis-
trative officer, I did not directly participate in activities): families visiting
Hebron prison, arrests, and patrols in the kasbah. But I often found myself
observing in what could be called a sort of "neutral" way. I watched with a
certain engrossed fascination, with an attempt to experience the mechanics of
subjugation, and I was fascinated with the way that the occupation finds its
expression on an everyday level, in everyday practices: soldiers checking iden-
tification cards; [Jewish] settlers' provocations; "locals" [Palestinians] com-
plaining about border policemen who had taken their ID cards; the
frightened eyes with which they sometimes looked at me; the arrogant stares of
many of the younger ones; members of my unit sometimes driving wildly in
jeeps; keeping my back to the wall while standing in the* suq *(market) so that
I would not be knifed; border policemen "handling" (hitting and kicking)
youths who had been arrested; the "expanded presence" of the IDF (more
guards, more patrols) during Jewish holidays.... And, during all of this period
I showed no outward distance from my military role. I accepted my role willingly and handled all of my administrative duties quite well. Was I only an
neutral observer of a fascinating social drama? Was I only a spectator?*

***

*After coming home from about three weeks of reserve duty in the Intifada I
encountered fatigue, apathy and disorientation. I feel very similar things
every time I return to civilian life from relatively long and intense periods of
reserve duty. Is this not an example in miniature of the "coming home"
syndrome that I have read about; the feelings of many Americans soldiers
upon returning from Vietnam?*

Personal journal, summer 1988

***

*During the summer of 1993 I visited the brigade commander in his home
for an interview. A member of the standing army, he had been trained as an
infantry officer from the beginning of his career. We talked about the special
characteristics of the infantry.*

> *The infantry has all sorts of problems that other corps do not have; at least not in
> the same extreme way as does the infantry.*

Q: *What do you mean?*
A: *All sorts of problems dealing with a civilian population that you have to
grapple with. Here you have to disregard all of the previous opinions that you had*

before. You have to be straight and stick to your aim or goal. You have to be loyal to the one that sent you and to your goal. Now as a commander of a reserve unit you are dealing with a much larger problem than in units from the permanent army. In the units made up of soldiers in their compulsory term of service you can disregard [private] opinions and say "Hey guys, we are all here and that's it." You don't have a problem of people coming from the agricultural sector or the economic sector or from the judicial sector; with reservists you just can't say that "nothing is relevant to us." You can't say "no discussion, no talking; and that is it." You can't.

Now I know that I am putting things in an extreme manner but with reservists it's much harder and you have a lot of temptations. It's not that other parts of the army don't have these kinds of problems, but that in the infantry it's in general much more serious.

Q: *Is it more serious because of the kinds of activities that infantry units are supposed to carry out?*
A: *Yes, yes. I think that you can find a morality of war [moosar milkhama] among the other forces, but that for infantry soldiers it is much more complex. When you fire a shell in a tank, or when you cast a bomb from a plane you don't have a concrete connection with whom you hit. And in the infantry you do have this concrete connection, more than others... In the infantry you have much more contact with enemy soldiers in a way that you can ask the question "could we have taken them as prisoners?" You face these kinds of questions much more than if you shoot at someone from far off either from the ground or from the air.*

5. ENEMIES

❧❦❧

To use a current anthropological term, *the* military other, the enemy has been altogether missing from my analysis up to this point. In this chapter I will deal with three issues: a 'folk' categorization of enemies which is based on their perceived threat; the rhetoric of emotional control which saturates talk about relations with enemy civilians; and a short comparative note on the depersonalization or dehumanization of antagonists.

Enemies, Seriousness and Prestige

The major "folk" categorization of enemies in the battalion – that is, the way soldiers and officers classify different forces they oppose – is derived from the combat schema. The criterion for categorization is the seriousness of the threat antagonists pose to oneself, to one's unit, and to the performance of both. This standard is derived from the combat scenario because of the knowledge that combat is a menacing, life-threatening situation. Enemies are thus arranged along a gradation of (decreasing) significance: regular armies, organized and professional Palestinian or Lebanese fighters, knife wielders, Molotov cocktail and stone throwers, tire burners and finally to "just" civilians demonstrating. The point is simply that a criterion derived from the key combat scenario allows the unit's soldiers and officer to place different kinds of opposing foes on an ordered continuum.

This continuum is related to a classification that is found in the general security doctrine of Israel in which enemies are ranged along a gradient of threat to the state of Israel (see Gal-Or 1988): regular forces (with differing capacities to threaten Israel), militias, armed political factions and irregular bodies of fighters. While most officers and soldiers may explicitly or implicitly "know" this official doctrine in the sense of being able to understand it if it were told to them, the "folk" continuum I refer to here is analytically distinct, and used in separate ways from, the more general scale found in the security doctrine. By analytically distinct I mean that there are certain interpretations and applications of the "folk" categorization of enemies that are not addressed (or only peripherally addressed) in the formal IDF doctrine (see also Helman 1993: 161).

Let me mention three points in this regard. First, enemies' positions on the continuum are related to different types of knowledge about the treatment accorded to them. In other words, different prescriptions for behavior are derived from the various categories of enemies. For example, whether one shoots (or obstructs, or arrests), or what kind of protective gear one uses (the type of helmet used, perhaps) are things that are dictated by the category of enemy one opposes in a specific situation. Some of these prescriptions are, of course, dictated by the commanders of the IDF, but given the variability and uncertainty of situations in which the battalion is deployed, many prescriptions are formulated "on the ground" by the unit's officers, NCOs, and soldiers. It is within this "leeway for interpretation" in the specific circumstances in which soldiers must act that the folk knowledge of troops and commanders comes into play.

Second, the continuum is used in ways that are similar to appraisals of training exercises. The continuum is employed as a measure of the importance of specific kinds of activities: the more dangerous and the more threatening a given operation, the more important it is. Thus a patrol along international borders (Lebanon or Syria, for example) opposite regular armies or professional fighters is more serious and critical than patrols in the occupied territories. For example, during the Palestinian Uprising, Ari the battalion commander often stated that maintaining regular military discipline, open lines of communication, and commanding are more important than all of the actual actions undertaken in the Intifada. While unstated, the reasoning behind these kinds of statements seemed to be that maintaining the unit's potential for military performance, related as it is to missions against "more serious" opposing forces than to the civilians of the Palestinian Uprising, was the commander's more general and significant purpose.

Third, the categorization of enemies that soldiers face forms the basis for a scale of prestige or stature accorded to an individual or a unit within the IDF and in (Jewish) Israeli society in general. Accordingly, participation in battles in war is more prestigious than participating in engagements during "peacetime". Both activities are considered more impressive than patrols along the borders where "nothing happens," and which are in turn more respected than policing civilians in the occupied territories. When we were scheduled to be deployed along Israel's north-ern borders opposite Syria for instance, many soldiers saw this activity as more rewarding and "serious" (*retsini*) than another stint in the Intifada. Again during this period at least two officers reported that they felt the missions along the border were more "real" (*amiti*), or that they had a "dimension of military work" there that they did not find during assign-ments in the occupied territories.[1]

The status hierarchy created within the Israeli armed forces – in such units as the battalion I served in – extends also to the manner by which different types of military activities and units are perceived and accorded social significance within Israeli society. In our (Jewish-Zionist) society, the type of unit in which one (or members of one's group) serves, and even the proportion of casualties suffered by the members of one's group, are seen to be proof of the "extent of one's commitment and the centrality of the group in the mainstream of society" (Aronoff 1993: 53). Thus position in the military (itself derived from participation in combat) determines to a great degree the kinds of status, prestige, and social significance accorded soldiers and officers. These kinds of notions are often formulated in humorous (if biting) terms. In the American army, reasoning about prestige and social importance is exemplified through the use of such expressions as "typewriter commandos" during World War Two (Kennet 1987: 129) or "remfs" ("rear-echelon motherfuckers") in Vietnam (Dyer 1985: 139) to refer to noncombatants. In the IDF, support level soldiers are often referred to as *jobniks*, i.e., people placed in relaxed and undemanding positions.

But what are the implications of such categorizations for operations in which the enemy is faced directly? As I went over my fieldnotes I was struck by the extent to which the "enemy" as a general category is discussed within the unit in terms of the machine metaphor. In briefings, planning meetings, and exercises the enemy is treated as a complex of equipment, men, and drills. The number and quality of the opposing forces, the types of ammunition and support groups they have, or typical maneuvers that characterize them are described and analyzed. Similarly, in any situation where enemies are to be potentially engaged, the problem, as the commanders see it, is usually one of simply finding the right means (*emtsa'im*) to handle (*letapel*, literally "treat") them. For example, during preparations for real or simulated missions, the issues discussed often involved deciding upon the right force composition, tactics, and ammunition for countering the perceived threat. Similarly, when talking about the effects of support artillery, soldiers talk about "attrition" (*shkhika*, literally "erosion" or "grinding") among enemy forces as though they were simply machinery. The same reasoning undergirds the "neutral" terms used to talk about 'interaction' with the enemy: engagement (*maga*), incident (*eru'a*), or skirmish (*hitaklut*).

A number of implications stem from this point. In the first place – and this may go against some received scholarly wisdom – images and concepts used in regard to oneself or one's unit can also be used for evaluating the enemy. Thus, paradoxically, just as one can talk about "throwing out" a soldier from the unit as some kind of useless implement, so one can talk about casting aside people who are "in the way" during the Intifada. Similarly, just as a commander can express admiration for the smooth operation of his force, so too he can speak approvingly of an enemy's handling of men and equipment. Accordingly, a common image or metaphor of "soldiers are like industrial things/objects" underlies conceptions of both friendly and hostile forces. A related (if uncanny) stress on how the enemy is "like us" is evident when soldiers use the "unit as brain" metaphor to talk about opposing troops. Commanders realize that antagonists operate under what they perceive to be their own conditions of uncertainty and have their own capacities for reacting to a volatile and threatening environment.

Civilians and Emotional Control

In the specific historical period during which I write the application of this pragmatic military knowledge is a fundamental concern for the IDF. It became a practical matter because it was during the IDF's Lebanese debacle (1982 to 1985), and even more so during the Intifada, that the problems of defining and reacting to civilians arose among the army's combat troops. These problems arose in ways that were dormant since the early 1970s when the Israeli military grappled with massive civil unrest in the Gaza Strip. To be sure, since its very inception, the IDF had to deal with "enemy" civilians. But except for limited periods such matters were usually relegated to special units of the IDF. What has happened in the past decade or so is the emergence among "ordinary" combat troops of a heightened awareness of the distinctive set of definitions and procedures necessitated by operation in civilian areas.

The following assessment is by Omer, commander of the support company. In my office at the Hebrew University a few weeks after our first stint in the Intifada in the Hebron area, Omer talked about the activities of the Palestinians:

> Hebron's on the whole rather quiet. In the [surrounding] villages they're much more organized, and they get organized much quicker... They're also much braver in the villages.... They perform (*ovdim*, literally "work") much better, perform with very good techniques; that is, they know every alley and every corner in the area. You come [into a village] and suddenly above you a whole lot of people will be throwing stones at you and suddenly they disappear.... They will catch you at your weakest points.

Another example is from a conversation I had with Ari, the battalion commander. We were talking about a town near Hebron when suddenly he put himself in the Palestinians' place:

> You know, the Arabs could wage an even more effective struggle than they do today. For instance, instead of throwing rocks they could just line up in the main street of a village and do nothing. Just stand there. We as Israelis would find it much more difficult to react to such types of struggles.

By attributing a combination of machine-like qualities and brain-like organizations to enemies members of the battalion (like Israeli soldiers in general) are able to perceive, and to act towards, civilians as though they are professional or semiprofessional soldiers. In this attribution, one finds a subtle conflation of the distinct categories of civilians and soldiers into one class of enemy. This conflation does not create a strictly new class of foe, but rather allows the reapplication of conventional metaphors (usually used in regard to regular soldiers) to civilians in the context of the Intifada. In this sense, the combat scenario as a model embodying what soldiering is about comes to govern a variety of situations that are not strictly military in essence. As Gal-Or notes in regard to the IDF in general, the same conceptualization that has been applied in the IDF in regard to regular armies is now utilized in various "engagements" with non-regulars and with civilians (1988:24; also Ben-Ari 1989). Two commentators, Zev Schiff and Ehud Ya'ari (1990: 155) have provided a sophisticated appraisal of the activities of combat units in the Intifada. They mention how "strange" they felt when they heard soldiers from elite IDF units speak proudly of stealing up to "enemy" houses at night (to gather intelligence) without noticing that they were talking ⸕ about ordinary civilian houses.

A typical illustration, taken from a period during which the unit served in the Palestinian Uprising, may illuminate the peculiar kind of attitude fostered towards civilians. (I have no comparable data on the Lebanese experience.) The following is a translation of a briefing by Ehud, commander of C company:

> So our missions define our activities [patrols and keeping roads free of stones and roadblocks]. This means we don't come in contact with them too much. This means not to go wild with live ammunition. Don't shoot plastic bullets. We don't usually fire. We will not provoke them (*nitgareh*), won't throw anything at them.

Eran (deputy of the support company) said of firing plastic bullets at Palestinians:

> There was once when I shot two plastic bullets and this was my greatest failure during the last five years. I made a mistake in going into the village and then I had to shoot two bullets in order to get out of there. It is a mistake to shoot live ammunition of any kind; it shows lack of control, and there is no need to put your finger on the trigger.

The following words are from a meeting held to conclude another tour of duty in the occupied territories. Ari the battalion commander was speaking:

> I know of only two accidents (*takalot*) of opening fire during this period. One was the guy who fired in the air, and the other was the soldier that fired during that night. I hope these were only irregularities (*kharigot*).... I don't think this should satisfy us because it still happens to us. As commanders these things keep happening and the responsibility is on us.

A platoon commander from another infantry unit was interviewed for a Hebrew newspaper (*Davar*) in Israel after serving for a month in the city of Nablus (in the northern part of the territories). He observed:

> It was a dangerous game. In the alleys we were scared of a knife; someone pulling us into an enclosure and knifing us. We used to go in the street in

groups of six with the person bringing up the rear wearing a bulletproof vest against a knifing or a shot. We always had to look back and maintain eye contact with that person.... The approach was professional. I never reached a situation where I lost control. We didn't take out any anger or resentment (*atsabim*, literally "nerves") on anyone. But when fifteen people came opposite me, surrounded me and threw rocks, I was a bit happy that I could identify someone who was throwing rocks and shoot him with a rubber bullet. It's part of the game.

As may be evident from these passages, a heightened degree of emotional control is required of soldiers dealing with civilians. Along these lines of thought, using "undue force" – that is, hitting, pushing, beating, or shooting – against civilians is considered an aberration. It is an aberration not just because of the basic humanity or human values desired of the soldiers, but no less importantly, these are aberrations because they indicate a lack of professionalism. Use of "undue force" is viewed as lack of control and an inability to master oneself and the situation.[2] Interestingly, however, from the perspective of the combat schema, the danger during the Intifada is not so much one of lack of emotional control leading to paralysis (although this is a possibility), but rather lack of such control leading to reckless and angry behavior.[3]

I am not arguing that incidents like hitting and shooting civilians do not happen. They happen all too often. What I am arguing for is an awareness of the *categorization* of these acts as exceptions, and for an understanding of the organizational implications of this kind of reasoning. Soldiers who cannot control themselves, and commanders who cannot control their troops (and themselves) are considered to be inept or nonprofessional. Under the logic of the machine metaphor these men are labeled as some "ill-fitting" or "mal-functioning" parts of the unit. Thus all one has to do as a commander is to replace these men ("mechanical parts") so that the battalion can continue to perform.

Depersonalization and Demonization: A Comparative Note

While a characterization of enemies as complexes of men and equipment and an emphasis on emotional control in handling antagonists are more than obvious on one level, I would contend that they are not universal military traits. By placing the case of my battalion (and that of the IDF in general) in a comparative perspective, I suggest a contrast between

Israel's army and other armed forces, or, to be more accurate, parts of armies in certain historical periods. While the definitions and categorizations derived from the machine metaphor in the IDF are related to a dehumanization, or depersonalization of the enemy, they do not express a demonization of the opposing forces. While depersonalization is essential for military performance because it allows the management of emotions during the execution of violent acts, such dehumanization need not necessarily be accompanied by a systematic, organizational vilification of enemy forces.

Antagonists are undeniably dehumanized when they become "objects" or "things" – so many targets to be hit, obstacles to be destroyed, pieces to be knocked out, or articles to be taken into account in the threatening environment. But in the context of the IDF (and here my assumption is that the battalion is representative of Israeli military culture in general), enemies are rarely vilified in a systematic and organized manner. The Israeli situation stands in stark contrast to the American forces which were characterized for long periods by an almost obligatory demonization of enemies and their portrayal as the foes of civilization and as the opponents of progress (Holmes 1985: 366; Cameron 1994). If scholars such as Fussel (1989), Cameron (1994), Dower (1986), Eisenhart (1975) and Shatan (1977) are to be believed, the "objectification" of the IDF's antagonists is different from the dehumanization of enemy forces that went on in the American army and marine corps during World War Two and the Vietnam War.

Kennett (1987: 155) suggests that during the Second World War Americans waged two different kinds of conflicts in terms of the military's definition of enemies. Despite all of the imputations of Nazi "barbarism," both armies tacitly acknowledged that the other was fighting in basic conformity with the rules of civilized warfare. The German soldier inspired no strong detestation. There was nothing particularly pejorative in the terms "Jerry" and "Kraut" (Kennett 1987: 156). In contrast, the strong animosity to Japanese soldiers was based on a combination of racism and religious legitimation (Ballard and McDowell 1991). Thus for instance, some American soldiers felt that Japanese troops did not have the "white man's feelings" and so were less sensitive to heat and other forms of physical discomfort (Kennett 1987: 167); and many saw these soldiers as "silent, cunning, a relentless and single-minded predator. They never saw the Japanese as being in any sense akin to themselves in feelings and emotions" (Kennett 1987: 168). Kennet cites a verse written by an amateur poet that is illuminating:

> Your code is the code of assassins
> Who stalk in the shadow of night.
> You learned a lot from the white man
> But – *you* didn't learn how to be white.
> (Kennett 1987: 163; emphasis in original)

Twenty years later, American soldiers' images of the Vietnamese enemy appear little changed from the stereotype of the Japanese enemy in the Second World War. The Vietnamese "were thought of as monkeys, insects, vermin, childlike, unfeeling automata, puny... inscrutable, uniquely treacherous, deranged, physiologically inferior, primitive, barbaric and devoted to fanatical suicide charges" (Shay 1995: 105). Against this background, it is perhaps not surprising that American soldiers had the (unofficial) "mere gook rule" which declared that killing a Vietnamese civilian did not really count (Holmes 1985). Indeed, American troops typically remarked that

> Charlie [the Vietnamese enemy] – he had no feelings. Charlie never cared whether he lived or died.... We'd shoot them, and y'know, they just didn't care. They had no concept of life.
>
> Then-n-n you run into somebody that you start firing at, and you say "Well I'm going to kick his fucking little fucking Gook Ass." (Shay 1995: 105 emphasis removed from original).

Shay's thesis is that in Vietnam (and by extension, in the Second World War in the Pacific theater) modern habits of nationalism and racism have blended with the biblical idea that God's enemies should be annihilated (1995: 114). His argument echoes the contentions of a number of other scholars who have noted that in holy wars and crusades the enormity of the enemies' denial of faith is central to the legitimation of violence (Kehoe 1989), and that American politicians have often systematically demonized the enemy (Dower 1986: Part II; Frank 1989: 180–81).

But what is more relevant from our perspective are the internal implications of these views for military organizations. Shay (1995: 103) relates images of the enemy to military instruction: "Vietnam-era military training reflexively imparted the image of a demonized adversary: The enemy soldier was pictured as evil and loathsome, deserving to be killed as the enemy of God and as God-hated vermin, so inhuman as not really to care if he lives or dies." Similarly, Grossman (1995: 162) suggests that while in the war against Japan, Americans had an enemy so different and alien that the military could effectively implement cultural distance (combined with a powerful dose of moral distance related to "avenging" Pearl Harbor), in Vietnam the primary psychological distance factor utilized was moral distance, deriving from America's "crusade" against Communism.

More concretely, the American forces seem to have systematically cultivated among their troops a rage against the Vietnamese foe. During Vietnam, rage at superiors fostered during training was transformed and channeled (especially among the Marines and the airborne forces) into fury at the enemy. Training practices at the time reflected a positive view of humiliation and degradation as motivational techniques (Shay 1995: 202). Indeed, the "logic" behind such practices appears to have been an attempt to demean and debase troops in a manner that could later be directed towards the antagonists in Southeast Asia. The "folk culture of the American military, especially during the Vietnam War, merged the fighting spirit with being berserk. Leadership beliefs [later, in and around battlefields] encouraged the conversion of grief into berserk rage as a militarily desirable consequence" (Shay 1995: 200).

The Israeli army, in contrast, does not encourage or value the berserk state, and generally refrains from extreme forms of humiliation as part of training for motivation or for the inculcation of a fighting spirit. This point, moreover, is especially true for the country's reserve forces who make up the foundation and the bulk of the IDF's strength. In my unit, and probably in most of the elite forces of the IDF, there is almost *no organizational* propagation of a view in which enemy forces are turned into "evil" groups deserving some kind of special, wrathful treatment.[4] For example, Holmes (1985: 282–83) cites an extensive research project on the IDF that found that very few soldiers mentioned hatred of Arabs as a motivating factor for fighting. Rather, the chief factors were references to the small, cohesive groups of combatants. Moreover, while it should be stated that Shalit (1988) found that hate and violence towards Arab enemies were problems among support troops (during the war in Lebanon) they were precisely those soldiers who were not trained for emotional control in combat. In Israel, the historical change in attitudes to the enemy were (arguably) the Six-Day War of 1967 and the Yom Kippur War of 1973. Israel's overwhelming victory in the former conflict may have led to a period of ridicule and contempt for the armed forces of the Arab countries. But after the Arab forces' success in the latter war, this disdain was reversed, and what emerged was a renewed regard and respect.[5]

If my contentions hold, then we may be able to understand something about the distinctive ways in which enemies are handled by different military organizations. Shay (1995: 118) is correctly aware that "any ideology that debases the enemy endangers the lives of soldiers while they fight." It is a dangerous ideology because it leads to a situation in which the strengths and advantages of the enemy are not taken into account by soldiers and commanders in a realistic manner. Reflective military commanders "have always rejected a positive image of the berserker, noting the degradation of unit effectiveness that comes from the berserker's loss of all social connection... [and because a berserk person has] lost the capacity for restraint" (Shay 1995: 200). Notice that at the base of Shay's argument is the model of combat in which the soldier's need for restraint, reserve and moderation of action are directly related to his (and his unit's) performance. But the obverse of his argument does not seem to hold. His contention is that the truth that veterans learned in Vietnam was that men cannot kill an enemy under-stood to be honorable and like oneself (Shay 1995: 103). Shay thus seems to suppose that because war cannot be waged on the assumption of a similarity between combatants and antagonists, then it inevitably leads to the latter's demonization.

Dave Grossman (1995: 92), who has gathered and integrated a very wide range of studies of killing, makes a similar argument:

> Even the language of men at war is full of denial of the enormity of what they have done. Most soldiers do not "kill", instead the enemy was knocked over, wasted, greased, taken out, and mopped up. The enemy is hosed, zapped, probed, and fired on. The enemy's humanity is denied, and he becomes a strange beast called a Kraut, Jap, Reb, Yank, dink, slant, or slope.

Grossman's rather persuasive reasoning is that inflicting violence in combat causes deep guilt and pain among soldiers, and that the language of warfare helps troops to deny what is really happening so as to make this violence more palatable. But here again, Grossman seems to believe that there is an imperative move from a language in which the imagery of enemies is one of "things" (to be knocked over or mopped up) to one in which they are "ogres" or "brutes" (a beast).

Both Shay and Grossman appear to conflate objectification of enemies with their demonization. To reiterate, both processes involve deperson-alizing the enemy, but they belong to (and are based on) different metaphorical worlds: objectification pertains to a universe populated by man-machine-drills complexes; demonization fits in a space inhabited by sinister and demonic beings with malevolent intents. While it is true that during World War Two (in the Pacific theater) and the Vietnam War both kinds of metaphorical applications were used together, this is not a predetermined necessity.[6]

Let me be clear about the implications of my argument. I do not argue that the process of depersonalization-through-objectification (enemies as machines) is more morally palatable than the demonization of antagonists. What I do contend is that this type of dehumanization allows a more rational (from the army's organizational point of view) treatment of the enemy. Holmes (1985) sums this point up by noting that without the depersonalization of the enemy during training, battle would become impossible to sustain. But if the abstract image is overdrawn or depersonalization is stretched into hatred, the restraints on human behavior in war are easily swept aside. If on the other hand, men reflect too deeply upon the enemy's common humanity, then they risk being unable to proceed with the task whose aim may be eminently just and legitimate.

I would proceed a step further than Holmes's insight. My suggestion is that the application of the *same* imagery and metaphorical language "to us" (to friendly forces) and "to them" (to antagonists) is necessary for soldiering. A psychological model developed by Rieber and Kelly (1995) may be instructive in this regard because it is based on exploring the meaning systems by which soldiering and enemies are defined. These scholars suggest that in stress-prone situations (such as medicine or law enforcement) a double process occurs; dehumanization involves two kindred but distinct processes. In the self-directed de-humanization, individuals protect themselves by immunizing themselves against stress-laden situations.

> Object dehumanization, the other side of self-dehumanization, describes the process and dynamics whereby the individual depersonalizes the other; enemification takes the process one step further and reduces the other to a "thing" that is potentially dangerous (Rieber and Kelly 1991: 16).

Self- and object-directed dehumanization, however, are inevitably heightened in situations where the threat of combat is present (Rieber and Kelly 1991: 17). Thus even in this period of technological war, "it remains true militarily that only ground troops can take and hold land. And soldiers who must fight these campaigns necessarily have a hands on relationship with the enemy and must develop emotionally virulent defenses against identifying with the humanity of the opponent" (Rieber and Kelly 1991: 17).

My analysis should be seen as an analytical complement to this psychological model. What I have shown in this and in the previous two chapters is a basic cognitive model or schema on the basis of which "self" *and* "other" are dehumanized through objectification (being turned into functioning machines). Put differently, while it is important to explain the psychological need for emotional distance from enemies, what my analysis provides is a specification of the meanings by which this distance is enacted.

Take the words of a British soldier during the Falklands War: "I felt neither hatred nor friendliness towards the Argentineans... I simply thought about the job in hand, and they happened to be in the way of getting the job done" (Holmes 1985:371). This short passage underlines the psychological process of distance *and* the meanings by which this process is established. To be sure, I am not arguing that my analysis is somehow more basic or important than the psychological insights, but rather that a nuanced exploration of how soldierly knowledge is organized in the combat schema allows us to understand the similarity and coupling between definitions of "our" and "their" forces.

Yet for all of the stress on the machine-like character of the unit, one must be wary of too simplistic a conceptualization of the men serving in the battalion. I now turn to deal with a number of issues related to motivation.

NOTES

1. Similarly, weapons are ranked along a scale of prestige on the basis of their singular importance in terms of accomplishing missions: machine gun, marksmen's rifles, rocket propelled grenades, grenade throwers, and the assault rifle.
2. Littlewood (1997: 11) makes a similar argument on a much broader scale when he notes that the "more a war (on the board game or toy analogy), with its declaration of hostilities, return of ambassadors, exchange of civilians and neutral inspection of prisoners, the more a professionalized military ethic is held in common by both sides, the greater the potential for the physical safety of non-combatants."
3. I am indebted to Denny Roy for this insight.
4. Perhaps a more suitable case for comparison with the IDF would be British soldiers in Northern Ireland and the kinds of highly controlled relations with their civilian foes that have evolved there.
5. In a related manner, a possible Israeli equivalent of America's holy war and the sacred legitimation of violence against enemies may be the case of the Gush Emunim movement in the Occupied Territories (Weisburd and Vinitzky 1984).
6. Thus in Vietnam, not only were the enemies vilified, but the language of objectification was used as well: they were reduced to little more than "pins on a map" or "blips on a screen" (Rieber and Kelly 1991: 17).

INTERLUDE 6:
A LETTER TO THE MEN

Shalom,

We have recently completed another combined activity. I would like to write to you to let you know a few things. I planned to talk about these things on the day we were demobilized, but in order to shorten the time before we went home, I decided to write to you.

I have been asked by all of the [military] elements that we have worked with over the past month...to let you know that they were satisfied with the way in which the battalion performed and with the results that have been achieved. The type of missions that we undertook are complex and demanding both physically and emotionally, and when you receive such feedback from people in such positions, that means that we executed our role in a good manner.

As most of you have heard, we have another stint of duty coming up in October. The ramifications are the following:

(a) Please take into account the fact that in life in general and in the army in particular, any plan changes according to changing circumstances. So treat this program only as a tentative plan.

(b) If we are deployed again in the Judea and Samaria area we will have to leave our political opinions at home again. Remember that we will be deployed during an election year [1992] and we will have to make a strong effort to look for what is common and unites us.

(c) Use your time until then in an enjoyable and efficient manner.

Be healthy and good luck.

Lehitra'ot *(see you)*
  Gavri Ben-Avot — CO Battalion

6. Models of
Motivation

*I*n both popular and academic writings, much has been made of the "spirit" of the IDF. Some scholars, such as Schild (1973), refer to the unique kind of organizational climate based on egalitarianism that characterizes Israel's armed forces. Others, such as Reuven Gal (1986), see the "fighting spirit" of Israeli soldiers as the crucial link between motivation and performance. In this chapter I deal with the relations between these three elements of organizational climate, individual motivation, and performance. These issues are important, because to gain a full understanding of soldiering, one must not be content with sketching the main cultural schema of combat. Without an account of how soldiers and officers conceive of the connection between this model and motivation we may have a sense of the cultural definitions of soldiering but we will not understand how these definitions are linked by these men to directive or motivational force.

There are two major "folk" models of motivation that characterize the men of the battalion: a causal chain predicating "need-fulfillment," which serves to explain and justify why commanders (usually officers) serve in the battalion and what they look for in service; and one predicating the creation of an "atmosphere" among the troops of each unit that underpins their willingness to serve effectively. While each model links individual motivation to performance in frontline units in a different way, both are founded on the basic combat scenario.

Need-Fulfillment

Let me begin with officers. In an essay about American reservists, Moskos (1988:48) perceptively noted that viewing reserve duty primarily as a kind of "moonlighting" activity is to miss a basic point. It is not so much economic or material benefits but other kinds of commitments that lie at base of the great deal of time – some compensated, some donated, and all voluntary – that men devote to their units.[1] In Israel, economic considerations are, relatively speaking, even less important for the majority of soldiers because most of them are compensated by the government (through their workplaces) to a level equivalent to their monthly income. Thus the Israeli situation bears a measure of similarity to the American one in terms of the nonmaterial benefits and commitments that lie at base of personal investment in reserve duty. While this point is especially true of officers who are part of the chain of combat command, it also holds for many technical and administrative officers, and for some senior and junior NCOs.

The battalion's officers, many of whom may serve over fifty or sixty days each year, often use phrases borrowed from the world of work to describe their future prospects in the unit. Many openly state that "they want to advance" (*lehitkadem*), or "that they are on the lookout for the promotion" (*ha-kidoom*). What kind of assumptions lie behind such confessions? My contention is that for a large number of officers in the unit – and most certainly for many other Israeli reserve commanders – military duty is seen as a sort of parallel or coinciding career.[2] By this conceptualization I mean not an alternative or optional professional career, but one carried out *at the same time* someone is pursuing his main (civilian) career. This model of careering, moreover, is based on a "fit" between the organizational requirements of the military and fulfillment of personal needs. For these men, career development in the IDF consists of a gradual progression into more authoritative positions, each of which allows them to meet certain personal challenges and to fulfil specific individual needs not met to a sufficient degree in their civilian lives and careers.

I begin with the general contours of this model of motivation and then spell out specific types of needs that are said to be fulfilled in the army. At one stage of my interview with Yoel, the former battalion commander, we broached the subject of ideology and personal needs. Yoel observed:

> There were times when I didn't understand this process and I thought I was doing things [reserve duty] for the good of the country. Later I understood that it's a personal need for me.... Any beginning psychologist will tell you this. I know I'm putting it in an extreme way, but the whole bit of "going [on reserve duty] for the good of the country" is a rationalization, something around which there is a [national] consensus. I learned this proposition about personal needs from that fellow who is a psychologist in civilian life who was my supervisor [*bakar*] at that exercise.... and at the beginning I argued with him because it all sounded so harsh [*boteh*].

Like many folk understandings of motivations, Yoel's interpretation gains force, and is legitimized, by being identified with expert knowledge (Helman 1993: 147). As Quinn and Holland point out (1987:9–10), in many contemporary societies, explanations of human behavior that are devised by groups of socially designated experts – in this case psychologists – come to provide models for making choices in, and for making sense of, the everyday world. The fact that these models are rooted in, and often formulated with the concepts borrowed from, the social sciences does not make them any less models on the "folk" level. This is an issue I shall return to later on in the volume.

Interestingly, Itai, the unit's deputy commander, also elaborated on the theme of fulfilling personal needs:

> Everyone has his own character, his own needs, I don't know how to define it, his own existential needs. I don't want to go into the psychological side of it because I never studied psychology, but I assume, a basic assumption without understanding psychology, that anyone who carries out a role in the army up from the level of deputy company commander, has a certain need. Ok? He does not do it [carry out the role] because he has no alternative. There is some sort of complementary relationship here between his personal needs and the needs of the army. These [personal] needs could be a lot of things like a need to control.

I asked him to be more specific:

> The truth is that I enjoy using power [*haphalat koach*].... Look, for example, when we went to that village: I had to prepare a plan; then you send the teams; you command them; you know what you want and what you get, a kind of finished product.... It's the same with a complex company exercise: complex in terms of command and control and in terms of the number and variety of forces you have. In short, it's a sort of integration of things, and I enjoy these things.

While the general model of motivation that Yoel and Itai seem to be talking about is one of need-fulfillment, the specific need both focus on is the need for control and management. Yoel elaborated this point when he talked of the challenges of commanding a battalion: "At the beginning there was more excitement [*hitlahavut*] from the battalion, more of a challenge and less of a routine. But after a while you've proved to yourself that you are able to control everything [*lehishtalet*]".

A closely related need has to do with seeking what Csikszentmihalyi (1975) has termed a "flow" experience: the focused attention on particular tasks that stretch one's abilities to the maximum. In less technical terms, this term refers to people who seek experiences in which their competence is tested to the utmost. Such experiences include mountain-climbing, car-racing or even chess. During these occasions, time seems to "stand still" and all of one's attention is concentrated on the task at hand. Thus Yoel noted of a highly successful maneuver:

> Now to stand there on top of a hill with the planes bombing the targets, and then us attacking.... And to stand there and to see that things are flowing and this really gives you a feeling that you are in charge of the situation and there is a payoff for all of your efforts.

The reasoning here has to do less with the managerial challenge of building a unit over time than with the specific test of manipulating a highly complex exercise (in a specific time and place) in which all of your expertise and abilities are utilized to their optimum. The excitement and satisfaction gleaned from meeting such challenges are complex, of course, because constructing a "good" unit is a precondition for carrying out successful maneuvers. Itai phrased this point in terms of the "absorption" provided by such military situations:

> There's a kind of stimulus here. The stimuli here are complex. There is stimulus in the actual preparation and in the performance of things like in exercises or combat. You "operate" [*maphi'il*] people and there are risks. So you see, I don't work for any ideology; it's more on this level.

The commander of the brigade evoked an image of the aesthetics of orchestration and making movies to get across what he meant by the experience he sought in various levels of exercises:

It's an orchestra that is very hard to conduct. And whenever you get to the level of a company or a battalion or a brigade [commander] then you have to use your imagination to picture everything and then plan it out. And when it materializes it's very enjoyable. It's thousands of details.... It's a whole picture; it's not just that someone runs; It's that he runs and enters and fires and others are there and everything fits into a larger picture. And each time it's a scene: one scene is the breach, and another is the entering, and another is the attack.... And then the whole puzzle fits together and it's a great intellectual challenge to fit everything together.

When it succeeds aesthetically then it means that it succeeds in terms of the overall picture and the planning. The perfect picture in the end is very aesthetically pleasing. Because, for example, if you planned that here you will have smoke [smoke screens] and here the soldiers will enter and fire and when you come to the field and you have smoke but there are no soldiers for the attack and then the smoke ends and only then do the soldiers arrive, then its not aesthetically pleasing anymore. It's not beautiful and it isn't worth anything. You feel it by yourself and you don't need anyone to tell you that it isn't good. You feel that something in this orchestra doesn't work.... This is the point about exercises.

War is another matter. But the point of exercises is where you train yourself and the whole system is oiled, and it will work, and it is quite a problem to synchronize all of these things.... And it's very complex because it goes down to the level of individuals like Gurevitch and Mamman, or Goldberg and Ben-Yehuda that have to run at the pace that the company commander dictates to them. That's exactly where it is. It's because each one has their own challenge, and your challenge is to connect all of their challenges; that the whole orchestra will work like it should.

Echoing similar themes, an ex-company commander noted that

the company is the first level that has some kind of independence and that lets you create things in it; plan them and execute them. This is a product, a creation of the company commander... Now when you do these things and when they are successful you enjoy it. It's like when you successfully carry out a company exercise, and especially if you take a company exercise that is quite complicated in terms of control, in terms of the dispersion of forces. In short, it is the integration of things and I enjoy it.

When he told me that he enjoyed himself during company maneuvers, I asked him whether it was the same kind of enjoyment as is found during a basketball game. He thought for a minute and then replied:

Yes, it's like winning in basketball.... but it's hard to compare them. The level of preparation is different, the level of complexity is different, and the

95

responsibility is much larger.... This means that there is no place to lose in this game; that is your aim. Your aim in this game is to win, and only to win. This is the way you plan it and this is the way you hold the briefing [with the men] toward it, so that you don't get into a situation in which you lose. There is no place to lose and because of that there is more tension here.

Other officers used such phrases as the "enjoyment of being able to actualize planning in reality," or "the fun of seeing things work." The need for the flow experience, then, can be satisfied according to these commanders throughout the different stages of an exercise from initial planning to the stage of actual execution: for them much of the challenge revolves around mastering organizational complexity and uncertainty under conditions of danger.

Similarly, another closely related kind of need fulfilled by army service is epitomized by talk about risk-seeking. One officer spoke of engagements and battles as being "the most exciting (*meragesh*), interesting and thrilling (*meratek*) game there is, and one in which it is perfectly legitimate to look for these things." A young platoon commander, Nachman, spoke of the envy he felt for those who had the chance of participating in an exciting engagement (*hitakloot*). Eran, the support company's deputy commander repeatedly spoke of the flow of adrenaline as something he looks forward to in engagements with the enemy and in other such dangerous circumstances. And, the brigade commander talked about the "feeling that soldiers have when they run and shoot. The feeling is that the adrenalin is flowing; and it's a good feeling".

Here again, as in the general model of need-fulfillment which integrates psychological terms so too the folk schema of risk-seeking is phrased in "scientific" terms: the flow of hormones engendered by the heightened excitement of hazardous situations. While there is some scientific corroboration of these assertions (in the face of danger the autonomic nervous system comes into play and adrenaline flows to quicken the pulse and to heighten the senses [Clark 1989:84; also Solomon et al. 1995]) what should be noted is not only the adoption of scholarly findings by "ordinary" people in the military world. What should be underscored is that in the folk model, the essentially descriptive and analytical thrust of the scientific theory is transformed into a normative or prescriptive force propelling military behavior. While "objective" scientific findings are used to explain one's behavior, they are also subtly transformed into justifications for risk-seeking.

Notice the similarity of my case to the kinds of motivations people cite in regard to participation in the nearly universal sports and games of danger. In all of these activities there is a strong element of *playing* with risk, i.e. meeting a challenging and highly engaging activity. All over the world, for little or no material gain, people walk into cages of wild animals, walk tightropes, climb steep mountains, jump from airplanes or dive in shark infested waters (Clark 1989:83). It is perhaps in this light that the claim that for some men army service is a prolongation of youth should be seen. Front-line units, in other words, are legitimate venues for continuing to seek the risks and thrills of late adolescence.

One more type of need cropped up in the conversations I had with the unit's officers: the need for status recognition. I should state however, that while many men mentioned this point, all of them stressed that it was not the primary reason for undertaking their role as commanders and officers. Yoel's attitude is rather typical:

> In civilian life it is quite complimentary [*machmi*] to me that people know I am a colonel [uses English word]. Until this day the Turkish supplier at the factory calls me "Mister Colonel". Now this is not the main reason [for becoming battalion commander], but it's certainly there.

Another officer referred to the "respect and status" [*kavod vema'amad*] involved in commanding men. A younger platoon commander referred to prestige as being "something extra, a related dimension," referring to how his role in a combat unit is perceived by members of society.

This is an issue mentioned in an earlier chapter: participation in combat and risk-seeking behavior are related to social stratification. Most societies give special rewards to their warriors. In Israel, as Horowitz and Kimmerling (1974) noted, contributing to the country's security represents a reward in itself because participation in the military defines the extent to which someone is in the "social-evaluative system of Israel." As my case shows, officers serving in frontline units continue to openly acknowledge this fact and relate it to their motivation for investing in reserve duty.

Gibush, Atmosphere and the "Ordinary Soldier"

A different model of motivation, one related primarily to cohesion, comes into play in regard to soldiers. Here the chain of causal reasoning centers on creating a certain social atmosphere or ambience of fellowship seen as crucial for inducing soldiers to serve willingly and efficiently. To be sure, scholars dealing with the military have long noted the importance of cohesion for the accomplishment of military missions (see Ingraham and Manning 1981; Gabriel 1987: 120; Greenbaum 1979). But my question is not related to the social dynamics by which cohesion is attained and maintained in small groups in the military. Rather, I examine the cultural understandings – the cultural schemas (or scenarios) – that underlie the men's insistence on the importance of creating cohesion.

Mainstream Israeli culture is of interest in this regard. Kellet observes that "the Israelis *regard* fighting as very much a social act based on collective activity, cooperation, and mutual support. The *sense* of mutual responsibility implicit in the doctrine has a corollary that is tactically constraining but psychologically of prime importance. In no circumstances may the wounded or the dead be left behind" (1982: 250; emphasis added). The issue thus becomes one of unearthing the kinds of assumptions and causal schemes that underlie this view of soldiering. Katriel and Nesher addressed this problem with an excellent explication of *gibush*, a mainstream cultural conception of sociality in Israel (1986; Katriel 1991).

Gibush, which literally means crystallization but in connotation is closer to "cohesion," is part of an elaborate rhetoric of cohesion in Israeli society. While the ethic of *gibush* traces its historical roots to the communal utopia of socialist Zionism, it has been important in the formation of mainstream Israeli culture and is found in the dominant social ideologies of this day (Katriel and Nesher 1986:222). This rhetoric is used in educational establishments, work groups, labor unions, political parties, youth movements, sports teams, and even in informal friendship circles and families. In Israeli schools, to give just one example, cohesion is seen to be so important as to govern the arrangement by which teachers (and not pupils) rotate between homeroom classes. This arrangement, it is believed, assures that the social membership of the classes remains stable and thus can lead to the creation of cohesive groups.

The *gibush* metaphor implies the stable integration of elements making up a crystal. In its social analogue, the internal strength and solidity of both the individual and the group flow from the unifying sense of belonging, of being securely together "in place." The "social ideal of *gibush* involves an emphasis on the undifferentiated collectivity – on joint endeavors, on cooperation and shared sentiments, on solidarity and a sense of togetherness" (Katriel and Nesher 1986:224). Thus to talk of a cohesive school class or a megubash sports team is to imply their internal resilience and vitality.

In the army the metaphor is used in two related senses: one related to individuals and the other related to units as social entities. On the one hand, *gibush* is said to be a precondition for, even a cause of, individual soldiers' willingness to continue belonging to a unit and to perform at their best. On the other hand, *gibush* is explicitly linked to the military performance of units; by creating a cohesive unit one creates the conditions for excellent performance. As understood by the men of the battalion, the schema of *gibush* has a strong causal logic. The end products of *gibush* are motivated individuals who want to be together and a tightly knit military unit characterized by egalitarianism, solidarity, and strong boundaries and *therefore* capable of successfully carrying out missions.

The following passage quotes one of the oldest soldiers in the battalion (now a clerk). We were talking about the relations between a cohesive (*megubash*) unit and the performance of military tasks and missions. The soldier's reminiscences about the time he contemplated leaving his company linked *gibush* to the combat schema:

> The company commander called me in and told me that he did not want to lose a soldier like me because it is around soldiers like me that other soldiers crystallize (*mitgabshim*). You have to understand this against the background of my performance. I think that in pressured situations like in Lebanon I never succumbed to pressure, and carried out all orders and missions in a quiet and calm way and made sure that they were properly carried out.

But just how is *gibush* created? The underlying model posits certain social circumstances within which "forces" (internal psychological motivations) emerge that will "propel" soldiers. The crucial variable is seen to be the creation of a proper social atmosphere (*avira*) to motivate the men. The reasoning is similar to the one Katriel and Nesher found in educational establishments: it is social activities outside of the army (like parties, outings, or picnics) or within the army (like celebrations or the ubiquitous coffee drinking sessions) that help generate the proper atmosphere.[3] An ex-company commander, Aharon, explained how he had "crystallized" his unit by doing things with his troops: "small things like giving them a night in town (*after*), holding a barbecue (*al haesh*), talking to them, inviting them to your home." All these activities, he explained, made them feel that they belong to a special group with a fate of their own.[4]

Another element in the creation of *gibush* involves weakening the rigors of hierarchy. When I asked whether there should be a separate table in the dining room for the company commander and the officers (when the company is in the field on its own), one platoon commander answered:

> There is no reason in the world for a separate table. As a platoon commander I always sit with my soldiers. I do this very intentionally in the same way that I help to change a flat tire and all of those things that, strictly speaking, I don't have to do.

A soldier described how a previous company commander had succeeded in creating an "atmosphere" in the company:

> It was pleasurable [*hana'ah*] to meet people, to go to parties in and out of the military, and to be together [*beyachad*].... He invested a lot in it, and I think it was important because he crystallized us [*gibesh*]. So that even if there were problems with your [specific] platoon commander then you still wanted to come [to the parties] it created a sort of commitment (*mechuyavut*) and it was nice.

Other soldiers talked of such things as "buddiness" (*sakhbakiyoot*), "comfortableness" (*nokhoot*), or "personal ties" (*kesher, khevre*). A young platoon commander complained:

> The bottom line is that when a soldier talks of the state of Israel, he isn't talking about the state of Israel but about his military company (*plooga*). What links him to this country is not a tradition or Jewish identity but the feeling of being one of the boys.

To clarify the earlier point that *gibush* seems to be a cultural theme particular to Israel and to its armed forces note the *relative* lack of hierarchical differentiation within the IDF's field units and especially among the infantry. That does not mean that the men do not recognize differences in rank and its associated responsibilities and privileges. But when compared to the armed forces of other industrial societies, there is much less emphasis on rank and hierarchy in the IDF. For example, as Michael Gal (1973) notes, while there is a sense of a dividing line (in Israel's elite units) between officers and soldiers, the NCOs do not usually appear as a special, differentiated group. A platoon commander evoked a picture of closeness and distance when we discussed sleeping arrangements:

> I still think that it's important that you [officers] have separate sleeping quarters. This doesn't meant that soldiers have to knock five times on the door before entering; but even though he can spend up to half a day in my room

if he wants to, soldiers do need to feel that entering our room is a little different from their own room.

Moreover, because this relative egalitarianism is seen as an ideal to aspire to, it is frequently used as a standard by which to appraise units and commanders. The following excerpt is taken from a conversation with Yehuda, an "ordinary" foot soldier:

> We tend to constantly inspect the company sergeant-major and his deputy, the company clerk and the company medic in terms of how much they take on themselves; how much they help with the tasks assigned to the company. The first thing they are tested on is their contribution to the little things like bringing the food on time, like bringing clean clothes, like making a fair allocation of leaves, like taking turns in helping during guard duty, like helping to man the communications center.

The second point involves the social locus of cohesion implied by *gibush*. At first sight it may appear that *gibush* is the functional equivalent of the "buddy system" found in the American and Canadian armies (Moskos 1975; Ingraham and Manning 1981: 7; Kellet 1982: 99), "mateship" in the Australian armed forces (Van Gelder and Eley 1986) or the "comradeship" of the British military (Richardson 1978: chap 2). However, in contrast to the buddy system, mateship, and comradeship *gibush* is *not* focused on a dyadic tie. In the IDF one may speak of a squad, platoon or company that is "crystallized," or occasionally of the NCOs of a company or the staff officers of a battalion that have this characteristic. But one cannot, properly speaking, talk of a crystallized pair of soldiers (or, for example, in schools of two pupils who are *megubash*). If I were to look for a closer analogy in other armies, it would probably be the general theme of "camaraderie." Hence, my suggestion is that while cohesion is central to armies around the world (van Creveld 1983), its has a specific cultural expression in each national setting.

The point to note in regard to the IDF – and again, this is a reflection of a phenomenon in Israeli society in general – is the ubiquity and the pervasiveness of *gibush* as a cultural theme. Perhaps more than in other armies, *gibush* is explicitly seen by officers and soldiers of front-line units as essential to the performance of military tasks. To reiterate, all of this does not imply a lack of cohesion in other armies.[5] Rather it suggests that in the IDF these matters are much more elaborated and explicitly used as criteria for evaluating military service. A platoon commander formulated the underlying schema rather explicitly:

The better the social circumstances a soldier has, the more his commitment to the NCOs and to the officers, the better the interpersonal relations, and the less the probability that problems of not showing up for the army service [going AWOL] will crop up.

Omer, commander of the support company, explicitly related *gibush* to the tasks to be carried out by a unit:

> A company is something very dynamic.... The *gibush* is something that is determined over many years. Every time they [members of the company] are together they become more crystallized and this creates a sort of happiness [*chedva*, literally "joy"].... Everyone finds his place and his friends and then they begin to want to be together and on guard together or go out on patrol together.

> The minute you don't have a nice atmosphere, it begins to express itself in discipline problems: not going out on patrols on time, not performing the patrol the way it is supposed to be performed, or the same for a lookout mission or a roadblock.

The brigade commander observed in a corresponding manner: "If you have serious social problems then they will always influence the combat effectiveness of the unit. You then have to see what is the problem and how deal with it."

NOTES

1. Moskos's objects of analysis are career soldiers who have decided to stay on in the reserves: "At a certain point, retirement benefits become a key incentive. But not to be underemphasized is the attraction of having an added non-civilian and non-routine dimension to one's life: the camaraderie of the unit, the outdoor life of annual training, and the challenge of leading young people. For a few career reservists, moreover, reserve training is a way to recapture part of one's youth or an acceptable way for breaking the monotony of family life. Very important, patriotic and service-to-country motive are openly and frequently expressed by career members of the reserves" (1988:50).
2. I would like to thank Boas Shamir for this idea.
3. The structure and dynamics of these coffee sessions reflect a purported egalitarian atmosphere: water and coffee are placed in a pot on a small gas head (usually brought from home by one of the soldiers). When the coffee has boiled, sugar is added to the ingredients and brought to boil a few more times. The coffee is then poured into

glasses so that both the amount of liquid and the froth are shared out as equally as possible. Drinking is almost always accompanied by talk stressing common problems and a shared past.

4. A closely related manner of creating *gibush* involves collective deviance and the practice that Shalit (1988: 134) translates as the "supplementation of equipment" (*hashlamt tsiyud*). During such "supplementation" it is perfectly legitimate for members of a unit to steal – food, ammunition or clothes, for example – from other units as long as the theft is seen to contribute to bettering the collective (not individual) conditions of the thieves' fellow soldiers.

5. Kellet (1982: 46–47), makes an important distinction:

> There is a difference between cohesion and esprit (de corps).... Cohesion denotes the feelings of belonging and solidarity that occur mostly at the primary group level and result from sustained interactions, both formal and informal, among group members on the basis of common experiences, interdependence, and shared goals and values. Esprit denotes feelings of pride, unity of purpose and adherence to and ideal represented by the unit, and it generally applies to larger units with more formal boundaries than those of primary groups. In essence therefore, esprit (or regimental pride) constitutes a filter through which the primary group is linked to the army, and the army is a legatee of informal, face-to-face interactions.

Interlude 7:
The Dividing Line Between
Officers and Men

⤳⤳⤳

*The following excerpt underscores the kinds of dividing line usually found
in the military establishments of other countries.*

*The rigid division of military organizations into officers and enlisted men, two
entirely separate hierarchies of people covering roughly the same span of age and
often, at junior levels, doing much the same job, is so universal that it is rarely
considered remarkable. Yet armed forces have the most meticulously stratified
system of rank to be found anywhere, and they positively flaunt it.*

*Among all the intricate distinctions of rank, it is the gulf between the officers
and the other ranks that is most distinctive and important. Army lieutenants at
the age of nineteen or twenty will normally be placed in charge of a body of
enlisted men who are older and more experienced than themselves. The army will
expect them to rely heavily on the judgement of their NCOs, but the final decision
and the ultimate responsibility is theirs....*

*The origins of the officer/man distinction are political and social. For most of
history, those who ruled the state and employed the army also commanded it.
Military leadership was not only part of their main job...it was also necessary for
their own safety. If they did not control the army, it could be used by those who
did to challenge their power. The profound social divide...is a relic of the military
organization of feudal Europe, in which the nobility specialized in leadership in
war, and it is probably broader than is strictly necessary – but the fundamental
principle of hierarchy is quite functional in military terms.*

*Armies exist ultimately to fight battles – the most complex, fast-moving, and
essentially unpredictable collective enterprises (not to mention the most dangerous*

and confusing) that large numbers of human beings engage in – and the purpose conditions almost everything about them. It guarantees them their high position in the list of priorities of every government (for historically the outcome of these battles has mattered greatly to the armies and their owners). It also explains why they are so different from other human organizations, and so similar from one country to another.

The government and society of the United States are greatly different from those of the Soviet Union, but their armies are so close in structure and in spirit that their officers, when they come into contact, cannot help recognizing their common membership in a single, universal profession whose characteristics everywhere are shaped by the demands of battle.

Gwyn Dyer, *War*

7. CIVILIAN LIVES:
EMOTIONS, CONTROL,
AND MANHOOD

*I*n this chapter I go beyond the confines of my case to re-read my empirical findings and to draw out two wider (perhaps speculative) themes related to my analysis. Placing my examination at the "micro" level of individual experience, I focus on how behavior that is internal to military service may be related to individuals' lives outside of it. Hence, I move from the level of cognitive models to offer a few reflections about people's actual behaviors and experiences. First, I suggest a number of ways in which emotional control within the army is linked to such mastery outside of it. Here I utilize insights into the emotional worlds of Israeli soldiers provided by Amia Lieblich (1989) in order to shed light on my findings. Second, I propose how the combat schema may be associated with certain ideals of manhood among (Jewish) Israelis. To the best of my knowledge, apart from rather scattered remarks no systematic work on the link between military service and masculinity or notions of manhood has been carried out in Israel. One exception is Sion (1997). Thus the suggestions in this chapter should be seen as a series of conjectures and hypotheses for further investigation.

Emotional Control and Civilian Lives

Observers have long taken for granted that there are close links between the military and the civilian sectors of Israeli society. As I mentioned in

Chapter 2, two groups of scholars have attempted to come to terms with the social implications of this situation. The first group have tended to focus primarily on the institutional level or the relations between elites, and the kind of *problematique* they have dealt with revolved around the capacity of Israel's political system to maintain democratic arrangements despite the demands of security considerations, the prominence of military elites in decision making bodies, and the allocation of resources to ongoing military efforts. The dominant conceptualization within this approach was on the relatively permeable boundaries between the civilian and military sectors of Israeli society and on the mutual influence and "dilution" of the more extreme orientations of both spheres (see Horowitz and Kimmerling 1974; Horowitz and Lissak 1989).

More recently, a second wave of scholars has begun to ask questions about how this situation has led to the militarization of Israel. For example, while Ben-Eliezer (1995a, 1995b) talks about "militaristic politics" and Kimmerling (1993) about "civilian militarism," Peri (1993) has coined the term "religion of security" to characterize contemporary affairs in Israel. Broadly put, the stress within these investigations has been on exploring how war and conflict are part and parcel of Israeli society. These scholars all ask how war is an integral consideration of state institutions as they impinge on the larger society (Kimmerling 1984, 1985). But as in the earlier school of thought, so here most of these analyses are placed on the macro level of ideology, resources, and social arrangements.

But what are the implications of this situation – of close ties between the military and civilian sectors of society – for individuals? What are the effects of these circumstances on the people (primarily Jewish men) who constantly move inbetween military and civilian roles? In Chapter 7 I mentioned the concurrence of the *gibush* concept in different institutions of Israeli society. At this juncture, I would like to discuss the combat schema and its significance for the personal lives of reserve soldiers. My argument is twofold: first, I contend that the emphasis on emotional control found within the schema should prod us to reflect about hitherto little explored aspects of the IDF; specifically about the different mechanisms by which the Israeli army (like any military establishment) attempts to cultivate and regulate the emotions of troops. Second, I argue that we need to consider how certain emotional attitudes fostered through military experiences "migrate" to individuals' civilian lives.

Popular discussions about military life in Israel often revolve around notions of personal challenges and individual achievement and satisfaction. Yet these ideas about how individuals regard their military lives should not be simplistically accepted as expressions of the meeting point between people and the reality of the IDF. Rather, these perspectives are the outcome of a rather constant and systematic organizational cultivation of emotional attitudes within the military. Van Maanen and Kunda (1989; also Bailey 1983), have carried out pathbreaking studies on the relations between formal organizations and what they term "emotion work." They suggest that a central concern for organizations is how to guarantee the involvement and commitment of members to organizational goals. As a consequence, modern organizations consciously and intentionally structure the "lived experience" of their employees through attempting to govern their emotions: "Rules governing the expression of emotions at work are an important part of the culture carried by organizational members and any attempt to manage [organizational] culture is therefore also an attempt to manage emotions" (Van Maanen and Kunda 1989: 46).

In more conventional industrial settings, emotions are governed (via a combination of positive incentives and negative control) in order to assure a smooth and efficient production flow. In newer, more service-centered industries like Disneyland, which is Van Maanen and Kunda's focus, the emotions (and by extension the body stance and attitudes) of employees are controlled and managed so that they provide dependable and pleasant service. The control of emotions in a given organization, then, is carried out in order to achieve organizational goals.

As members of military institutions, soldiers too are open to a cultural management of feelings and sentiments. Accordingly, the feelings and sentiments of soldiers are managed and monitored in a manner that will allow them to perform and achieve military tasks (as we have seen, essentially to accomplish combinations of destruction, domination, and defense). But the military is peculiar in this respect, for the regulation of emotionality is carried out on two levels. On the one hand, it is administered in the processes by which feelings are mobilized *toward* the achievement of tasks (that is, in motivating soldiers). On the other hand, emotions are regulated *within* the tasks themselves. They are regulated because of the centrality of mastery or control of sentiments and passions to the accomplishment of military missions.

But the question becomes much more interesting if one asks about how "emotion work" learned and accomplished in the military is carried over to other contexts. Shay (1995: 150) in an insightful observation notes, "I speak of armies and families as creating social power, because the hold that each of these institutions has over its members comes to greatly exceed its moment-to-moment capacity to reward or punish and usually persists long after significant practical affiliation has ended." If military establishments do indeed have this kind of "social power," then this power may affect the experiential bases of certain aspects of Israeli men's emotional carriage and deportment. On the basis of work in Gestalt groups that she has carried out, Amia Lieblich, a professor of psychology at the Hebrew University, suggests that (Jewish) Israeli men tend to be nonexpressive in the emotional sphere: Israeli men frequently repress their feelings of pain or inadequacy and demonstrate a facade of omnipotence and invulnerability. Other men, according to Lieblich, often experience conflicts between a commmitment to be heroic and strong and natural tendencies to be weak and in need of support.

> I propose that the price for the facade of the strong, decisive man is a certain emotional detachment, lack of sensitivity to oneself and to others, and a restriction of spontaneity – traits which several men in the groups I led reported as bothersome. (Lieblich 1989:111)

In her book *The Transition to Adulthood During Military Service* (1989), Lieblich hypothesizes that from a developmental point of view, the formation of this kind of adult personality is related to the experience of war and military service. This kind of personality may, of course, be viewed as a functional prerequisite for the Israeli war machine. It is such a prerequisite because it allows men to function under the extreme conditions of battle in a manner that is unimpeded by excessive emotionality. But it would be useful to ask just how military service effects this kind of change in men.

I suggest as an extension of Lieblich's hypothesis that for many men (primarily, but not only, combat troops) "nonemotionality" or "lack of sensitivity", or "restriction of spontaneity" are related to the kind of emotional training – Van Maanen and Kunda's "cultural management" – imparted to soldiers in the army. In the military they enter a milieu in which they are appraised by others and appraise themselves according to a set of criteria centering on emotional control derived from the military's prototypical scenario: the model of combat. These criteria, moreover, are used during the compulsory term of three or four years of national service, and (as I have demonstrated throughout this volume) for extended periods every year thereafter during reserve duty.

How is this control learned? Given the locus of my analysis, what I can offer here are only a series of conjectures. My contention is that we need to consider emotions as cultural products that are reproduced in individual forms as embodied experience (Abu-Lughod and Lutz 1990:12–13). Soldiering according to this view, literally embodies a certain set of emotional attitudes to the world. "To learn how, when, where and by whom emotions ought to be enacted is to learn a set of body techniques including facial expressions, postures, and gestures"[1] (Abu-Lughod and Lutz 1990:12–13). Along these lines, in Chapter 4 when I dealt with the notion of *kor ruach* or "cold spirit" (the ability to act with confidence, poise and composure under trying circumstances), I pointed out that it includes such things as control of breath and voice while talking, giving orders smoothly, thinking clearly, reacting quickly, or even controlling one's limbs or countenance. Similarly, in Chapter 5, I gave an example of how an officer rather proudly told me of his self-control.

Much of the manner by which soldiers and commanders learn to embody emotional control is implicit and often related to unconscious following of models (either of respected commanders or of peers). But in addition, men are also constantly given explicit reinforcements for their behavior either through direct encouragement (or sanctions) or through the promotion (to more senior positions) of soldiers on the basis of criteria derived from the combat model. Moreover, Jewish-Israeli youths continually undergo processes of vicarious socialization (watching movies and television programs, listening to radio shows, or participating in various preparatory courses for the military) and anticipatory socialization (talking to older people who have been or are going through military service). Such presocialization includes a variety of projects such as the formal premilitary training received by youths in schools, prepatory meetings and briefings with representatives of different military units (the latter are invited onto school premises), or visits to military bases. Closely related activites are individual-centered preparations through physical exercises (and the emotional steeling these often entail) or the simple if significant, gathering of information on such matters as the conditions of entry into different units, the circumstances of services, and the criteria and opportunities for promotion.[2]

The result of the military experience is the development of what may be termed an "occupationally conditioned habitus" (McElhinny 1994), which involves a combination of a stress on performance and an "economy of affect." "Habitus" is a concept developed by the French anthropologist Pierre Bourdieu to describe how accumulated experience structures interactional behavior. Habitus is a system of lasting transposable dispositions which, integrating past experiences, functions at every moment as a matrix of perceptions, appreciations, and actions (Bourdieu 1977: 82–83). It is history turned into nature: the actual experiences of individuals are incorporated into memory, to form the common sense with which people's expectations about, and reactions to, subsequent incidents are shaped. The point to note, however, is that this "memory" is not only a cognitive function, but one grounded in people's very bodies and emotional postures. Bourdieu tends to emphasize the role of family and school in establishing the individual's stylistic repertoires of such attitudes to the world.

I would go further, following McElhinny (1994: 165), to suggest the central role of occupations – specifically the role of soldiering – in shaping the norms and internalization of appropriate expressions of affect. This point implies that through the various activities of the military (such as preparing for service and then participating in training or carrying out missions) men learn to be soldiers in the sense of embodying certain attitudes and stances. The power of the Israeli military is thus not only related to preparing soldiers for combat. No less importantly, it involves inculcating in men certain emotional stances to the world.[3]

Emotional control is characteristic of men undergoing military service in any of the armies of the idustrialized democracies. But the near universality of compulsory service for Jewish males and the continuity of service throughout their lifetime tend to make this kind of emotional regulation both more widespread and more subject to periodical reinforcement. Hence, at the risk of overstressing my argument, I would emphasize that control of emotions is not only the product of the initial period of compulsory service (on which Lieblich and most commentators focus), but is reinforced every year in the reserves. It is as though, to give what is perhaps an outlandish example, Israel were populated by a large proportion of men similar to the American drill sergeants examined by Pearl Katz (1990). In sum then, "cool" performance as embodied emotions is simultaneously phenomenologically experienced, positively reinforced and rewarded, and carried over into men's private lives.

Becoming a Soldier: Becoming a Man

But "cool" performance also encapsulates much of what it means "to be a man" for soldiers of the unit, as for many Israeli men, because a discourse on emotionality is at the same time a discourse on gender (Lutz 1990:69). This suggestion is more specific than a proclamation found in scholarly literature that the warrior is still a key symbol of masculinity in Western societies (Morgan 1994). My contention is that the combat schema is also a schema for achieving and reaffirming manhood. The term "manhood" refers to the main ideals or conceptions of approved ways of being a Jewish male in Israeli society (see Gilmore 1990: 1). "Ideals" refers not to a set of psychological traits that individuals may or may not possess, but to a group of culturally available, recognized, and legitimate themes that are more or less identified with certain aspects of being a man in a given society.

In his wide-ranging book about comparative aspects of masculinity, David Gilmore (1990) advances two interrelated ideas – one about the assumptions at base of ideals of manhood and the other about the means for achieving them – that are pertinent to my analysis. His first proposal is that the core notion related to being a warrior is the acceptance of men's expendablity. The idea is that to be men, individuals must accept the fact that they are dispensable. In fact, in many cultures the acknowledgement of one's expendability constitutes the basis of the "manly pose." Recognition of this social truth often "constitutes the measure of manhood, a circumstance that may explain the constant emphasis on risk-taking as evidence of manliness" (Gilmore 1990: 121). From a social point of view, Gilmore goes on to contend, ideals of "real manhood" should be seen as inducements to carry out collective goals because of the universal urge to flee from danger. In this sense, manhood ideals make an indispensible "contribution" to the continuity of the nation-state by encouraging men to act according to a code of conduct that advances collective interests by overcoming inhibitions.

In Israel, notions of expendability are explicated and legitimated through a profusion of stories, sites, and rituals devoted to heroism and sacrifice. Frequent wars have forced Israel to mobilize young men to fight in its armed forces. As a consequence, since the establishment of the Israeli national entity, it has been necessary to construct what Mosse (1990) calls the "myth of participation in war." Israeli society has consistently glorified military service, and especially battles, and developed a set of myths about courage and personal sacrifice (Gal 1986; Sivan 1991), cultural sites commemorating fallen soldiers (Kalderon 1988; Meiron 1987; Bruner and Gorfain 1983; Schwarz et al. 1986), and rituals marking the importance of war for the very survival of the nation-state (for example, Liebman and Don-Yehiye 1983; Handelman and Katz 1995; Handelman and Shamgar-Handelman 1997). Through these various ceremonies and accounts, ideals of manhood (expendability) are linked to wider notions of legitimate national goals and to the endurance and maintenance of the state through the constant sacrifice of individuals. Moreover, as Lomsky-Feder notes (1992), it is easy for young people to identify with these stories of heroism since they also incorporate attributes of masculinity such as grit, unyielding adherence to goals, ability to withstand physical and emotional pressure, and loyalty to friends. This level of cultural representation is important for showing how ideas of heroism resonate with ideals of manhood, but it is not enough, for in order to understand how "one becomes a man," one needs an explanation of how these ideals can be accomplished.

Here David Gilmore's proposals about how manhood is something that is achieved, attained out of constant efforts, is fruitful. Across many cultures,

> there is a constantly recurring notion that real manhood is different from simple anatomical maleness, that it is not a natural condition that comes about spontaneously through biological maturation but rather a precarious or artificial state that boys must win against powerful odds...a critical threshold that boys must pass through testing (Gilmore 1990: 11).

To pass these tests of manhood, boys must steel themselves, and must be "prepared by various sorts of tempering and toughening" (Gilmore 1990: 223–24). In Israel, it is in the interrelated elements of testing and tempering that military service and the combat schema are pertinent. If the prime trial of men, the chief ordeal for achieving manhood, is that of mastering stressful situations, then the fire fight is the epitome of such tests. Being able to act as a soldier in battles thus encapsulates the notion of a man mastering a stressful situation, and, if successful, of passing the test (see Sion 1997). It is in this light that I would suggest looking at the model of combat as a model for soldiering as well as for manhood.

Why is this so? In Chapter 4 I argued that in the highly stressful situation of combat a whole "rhetoric of emotional control" emerges. Here I contend that this emotional control —within and later outside the combat situation – comes to figure in a key model of masculinity. In the combat situation emotions take on prime importance for soldiers and commanders. In these circumstances, fear, apprehension, dread and at times exhilaration blend together and issue forth within oneself *because* of the external situation. The problem becomes one of agency: who will be master, situation or person, circumstances or man? Along these lines, the ultimate test of manhood, the prototypical trial is the fire fight. But the red badge of courage, the emblem of manhood, is less the wound than in being in a pressured situation and performing within its stressful circumstances by mastering one's emotions.

But, again, things are more complex. Only a minority of men participate in field units and only a smaller minority actually participate in various kinds of fire fights (in wars, engagements, or other kinds of combat). Here my contention is twofold. First, the link between the combat schema and the model of achieving manhood may explain the eagerness of many men to participate in combat as their ultimate test as soldiers and as men. Second, military service provides a hierarchy of situations that are based on the similarity to the combat situation. Thus there are a host of simulations of the combat scenario in which individuals can perform, be tested, and prove themselves as men.

Military service is actually made up of a "series" of tests of manhood and soldiering. These trials include not only battles or skirmishes (although these are the most serious ordeals). No less importantly, they include basic training, professional education (gunners, drivers, or snipers routes, for instance), various courses (NCO and officer training, for example), and various kinds of maneuvers and exercises. Because all of these events include simulations based on the model of combat, they are used to inspect and verify the characteristics and abilities of men. Put somewhat crudely, if one keeps one's cool and performs under such situations, then one is a man. To reiterate, military service resonates with wider ideas about national, state goals, but we also need to understand it as the scenario, the behavioral locus, which allows men to achieve manhood.

In fulfilling their obligations, men stand to lose in ways that are thought to separate them from women and boys. Because manhood is the male version of adulthood, one of its key features is the defeat of "childish narcissism" (Gilmore 1990: 223–24), a struggle against regression. It is against this background that we may understand why we hear so much talk among men in the army not only about not being women, but no less importantly, about not being children. Chapter 5 presented an example of how the deputy commander of the support company appraises a platoon commander in his company:

> He is an officer, he has emotional maturity, and he knows how to lead people, how to give orders, and he knows to distinguish between what is important and unimportant... He isn't a little boy who will cry every time he has to go out on patrol like some of these other guys we have in the battalion.

Here and elsewhere children are invoked as the contrastive class of people whose behavior is inappropriate to men. In a variety of situations soldiers are exhorted "not to act spoilt," and "not to behave like babies," or they are advised before patrol that "summer camp is over, now is the army." According to my data, more rarely, and in contrast to the U.S. Marines, for example (Eisenhart 1975), is the contrastive category that of women. Categorizing someone as a child in the circumstances of the unit thus allows the categorizer both to point to a desired set of behaviors suited to men and to negatively label the person being categorized.

In this sense, much more than the stretch of compulsory service, reserve duty represents the periodic creation of an exclusive male preserve: a recurrent creation of an enclave of space and time within which the meaning of military service and manhood is crystallized anew. If compulsory service is marked by a series of rites of passage, reserve duty underscores to a great degree how service also involves rites of affirmation; by periodically reliving their military "selves" soldiers affirm their identity as military professionals and as men. During stints of reserve duty, men are actually and symbolically "torn away" from their everyday civilian lives to participate in a public occasion in which certain key values are validated and personally experienced. Also validated anew are the values inculcated during youthhood. To put this point somewhat picturesquely, the image is of twenty-, thirty- and forty-year old men who periodically return to their eighteen- and nineteen-year old selves.

Such a conceptualization may cause one to reinterpret the taken-for-granted nature of reserve duty among large segments of Israel's Jewish population. Specifically, it may contribute to understanding some of the reasons for the continuing willingness of reserve soldiers to cede their time, energy and private activities in order to participate in actions that may at times be quite dangerous (Helman 1993:145). While from an individual point of view, reserve duty allows many men to actualize anew images of manhood, from a broader organizational point of view, these images can be seen as a major motivational force (Sion 1997). The military uses the imagery in order to assure a steady stream of willing and committed soldiers that will carry out its various missions and tasks.

One more point should be addressed at this juncture. In a convincing essay, Morgan (1994) suggests that we talk about a plurality of masculinities. Alongside the trials of combat are tests of manhood that have not been examined in regard to the Israeli military. I refer to the manner in which soldiers are inspected for doing their job, for applying their professional expertise and skills. National service can be seen to actualize another set of ideals of manhood; that of becoming a man in the sense of being able to succeed in the workplace as a craftsman, technician, or manager. In terms of the army, these versions of manhood are subordinate to the warrior ideal. We must recognize that there is not simply a diversity of masculinites, but that these masculinities are linked to each other hierachically. The warrior ideal, then, is the hegemonic masculinity (Morgan 1994).

If we conceptualize military behaviors such as control, risk seeking, or aspiring to tests, as something that many Jewish Israeli men have been socialized to carry in their "heads" (as key models and schemas) and in their "bodies" (as embodied emotions and attitudes), then we can ask questions about how cultural codes learned in the framework of their military experience are activated in a variety of contexts outside of the army. Such a formulation allows us, for example, to ask how such models have "travelled" from the military to the Israeli workplace to create what could perhaps be called an "Israeli managerial style." Or, to give another example, how they have "commuted" into people's leisure pursuits. For instance, in the past decade or so, upon the completion of their compulsory term of service, many Israelis tend to go on extended trips sometimes lasting a year or two to such places as South and Southeast Asia and Latin America. Yet there is an interesting point to these journeys, which can be seen as a sort of rite of separation from the compulsory part of military service. These travels very frequently include treks that are carried out in a "military" mode including precise planning, walking in small cohesive groups, and repeated tests of people's abilities to withstand hardships and to take risks.

As noted at the beginning of this chapter, the control demanded of men within the army tends to be reinforced by, and to reinforce, wider notions of self control as a central element of manhood in Western industrialized societies (Brandes 1980: 210). This is not surprising, since in such societies – and Israelis belong to such a society – there is a strong link between rationality and masculinity. As Haste (1993: 90) observes, "a central metaphor of rationality is mastery – over the environment, over others, and over ideas." What is problematic for Western men in general, in various personal and occupational realms, is intensified by the social contexts of the Israeli army; i.e., men must display control and mastery within public arenas of small, relatively cohesive, groups and often in close relations with commanders. Consequently, my argument is for understanding many aspects of Israeli society in terms of mutuality, of recursive feedback between the military and civilian parts of people's experiences. The military does not just train men, or dispose them to think and act in a certain manner once they are civilians. To be successful, ideologies must appeal to and activate preexisting cultural understandings that are themselves compelling. In the IDF, Israeli myths of heroism and Western notions of mastery and rationality reinforce each other and are actualized in the specific contexts of military units.[4] Thus the army invokes wider cultural understandings about manhood, and in this manner it feeds back into and energizes these same ideals.

NOTES

1. For example, rather than thinking or speaking the respect (*gabarong*) that helps reproduce a gender hierarchy on Ifaluk atoll in Micronesia, girls follow the curve of their mother's backs in embodying the bent-over posture of respect (Abu-Lughod and Lutz 1990:12–13).
2. Lieblich and Perlow (1988: 67) give a rather typical example of a soldier who went on to an elite scouting unit: "I prepared myself as best I could. I jogged. I worked out. I walked long distances. I got advice and some helpful tips from friends. Small things...."
3. Hence, hegemony is quite literally, as Bourdieu and others show, "habit forming" (Lock 1993).
4. One may well ask about the manner by which the "traditional" image (or myth) of the Jewish man who is caring, warm and not afraid to show emotions is related to this rather controlled military "man." In the context of my fieldwork this never directly entered into conversations with the men of my unit. Nevertheless, I would suggest that historically speaking, the contemporary image of the Israeli military man developed out of the image of the pre-state pioneer (*halutz*). This latter image (with its emphasis on directness and lack of emotionality) was based on the *rejection* of what are taken to be the stereotypical characteristics of the Jewish man of the Diaspora. As a consequence, the ideals of manhood we now know as mainstream Jewish "Israeli" constitute a renunciation of the imagery attendant upon Diaspora Jews but are mediated by representations of the historical pioneers.

INTERLUDE 8:
STRAIGHT TALK
AND FEELINGS

The "plainness" of dugri *speech is not the absence of style but rather an alternative stylistic option, which derives its force from the contrast between words, talk [diburim] and deeds [ma'asim]. In this dichotomy diburim is often qualified as* stam *[mere talk] and* ma'asim *are interpreted as socially oriented action, manifesting full commitment, in the spirit of the nation-building ethos to which this cultural contrast should probably be traced (Katriel 1986: 25).*

The war did not change the conventional style of command in today's IDF – the tough commander, rigid, that does not talk much, that answers "negative/affirmative" and is very professional. Today's IDF is a very modern system, in which there is a growing specialization. A commander today needs a greater amount of information than he needed ten years ago. This fact drives certain people toward "over-professionalization." The other issues to which he devoted himself ten years ago – education and values – he leaves to others: to educational officers and to psychologists. He is hesitant to deal with these issues, and that is why he creates an image of someone who constantly deals with professional matters, and is not accessible to the creation of ties beyond the professional domain. (Brig. General Avi Zohar, Chief Education Officer, quoted in Rich 1993: 176.)

I propose that the price for the facade of the strong, decisive man is a certain emotional detachment, lack of sensitivity to oneself and to others, and a restriction of spontaneity – traits which several men in the groups I led reported as bothering (Lieblich 1989:111).

8. CONCLUDING CONSIDERATIONS

*L*et me begin with a story. As my fieldwork progressed, and as I occasionally discussed my project with soldiers and officers, some men joked with me about feeling that I could somehow "peer into their minds." By these mild jibes these men seemed to comment about the fact that I had somehow come to understand and to explicitly formulate their doubts and reasonings. Perhaps they seemed to be wary of my "magical power" as an anthropologist, a power akin to the one psychologists have in the popular mind. From an analytical point of view, these kinds of reactions could be taken as an indicator of the validity of my findings; our discussions were a sort of "natural experiment" that tested my intitial interpretations.

Of course, I could not peer into their minds (unfortunately, I still can't). Rather I attempted, as an anthropologist, to look systematically at the publicly shared symbols, such as naturally occurring metaphors, images, and utterances soldiers use to give meaning to military life. Beyond using my own native intuitions and perceptions, I attempted to uncover the means (again, the words, tropes, and imagery) through which these men represent themselves to themselves and to others. At bottom, this is the analytical thrust of this volume. As an anthropologist, I did not analyze doctrinal knowledge of strategy or of tactics, or the expertise needed in drills and exercises. The subject under study was the meanings of soldiering and commanding as they are expressed and used in the everyday lives – in a taken-for-granted, common sense manner – of troops and commanders. This volume thus exemplifies a way of looking at military knowledge and at the way this knowledge is related to such notions as "conflict" and "combat," "soldiering" and the "enemy." A number of points follow from these assertions.

The first point is that much of military knowledge is organized around what I have termed the combat scenario or schema. Rather than being a fully ordered and coherent model, this schema is a set of basic themes – some contradictory, some complemintary – that form bases for the definition and evaluation of soldiering and commanding. In other words, such scenarios operate to designate much of what is considered normal, proper, and excellent in military life. Like all folk theories, the combat scenario is not "believed" in the sense that conscious theories are believed, instead it is *presupposed* as the occasion of thought or communication demands (Linde 1987: 362). For example, the presupposition that enemies are objects allows Israeli soldiers to handle them (in certain situations) as obstacles in the way of a smooth running machine.

Two, the power of this model, again like all folk models, lies in its summarizing nature; its reduction and encompassment of a great deal of information into a few simple themes and causal relations expressed in metaphors. Experience, as Ortony (1975) reminds us, does not arrive in little discreet packages but flows, leading us from one state to another. Metaphor allows the invocation of chunks of characteristics in a word or two. The use of metaphor communicates in an economical way what would otherwise entail listing long catalogs of characteristics. Thus metaphors of soldiering as they are organized in the combat scenario allow military people to evoke at a single stroke, in a single instance, a mass of characteristics related to service and performance. This quality of the model allows people to decide rather quickly and economically whether and how someone fits (or does not fit) the characteristics and attributes required of soldiers and commanders. The theoretical point here is that there is an efficiency inherent in "scripted knowledge": the use of scripts for often repeated encounters frees the individual's attention for other issues.

Three, the power of these models also extends to their generative capacity; their use in explaining, and extending knowledge to, new situations. For example, the Intifada was defined (and reacted to) in the same terms military men interpret "routine" situations where enemy forces made up of professional armies appear (Ben-Ari 1989). In this sense, the combat schema and the models of motivation are frameworks for interpretation and not sets of routines people automatically follow. While I have only marginally touched upon this issue in the present volume, it should be stated that it is especially in new situations that the power of commanders to construct the reality of the units they lead is evident. These people have this power because it is primarily they who provide the terms through which the military organization and its threatening environment are understood.

Point four is that the models are linked to concrete prescriptions for action. The folk models of soldiering predicate (whether implicitly or explicitly) certain causal schemes dictating how to inculcate valued (or eradicate vilified) practices and attitudes. It is these purported causal chains that undergird assertions about violence, functioning, performance, and the creation of cohesive units. In other words, my analysis should not be seen as just another exercise in delineating the ideational forms of discourse about soldiering. Its focus is also on social action and practice. An analysis of these models thus entails not only uncovering the assumptions underlying how military things are reasoned about, but also make explicit the causal assumptions involved.

Five, folk models need not – indeed should not – be thought of as presenting a coherent or globally consistent whole in a way that an expert's theory is designed to be (Quinn and Holland 1987: 10–11). Rather, they are shared schematizations that while being internally contradictory show a certain thematicity in organizing a given body of knowledge. I stress the words "certain thematicity" in order to underline the fact that such schemas may be simultaneously seem both internally inconsistent and evince some congruity[1] (see Appendix III). One example is the incongruity between the machine metaphor and the requisites of *gibush*, i.e., between soldiers as dispensable parts and the special quality of cohesive relations between irreplaceable members of a unit. In part this contradiction is related to a wider inconsistency between the image of a machine as impersonal, non-feeling, and uncreative and other dimensions of Israeli military service that include the affection and closeness of soldiers.

My aim is not to fully clarify and resolve these kinds of contradiction but only to point to the fact that they are part of the ongoing knowledge of military life. Thus the existence of such inconsistencies is not (the desires of certain social scientists and military people to the contrary) a case of unclear thinking, but rather the way practical thinking is organized. As Sjoberg and his colleagues note (1991: 51), "So committed are some survey researchers to the principle of consistency that they often assume that inconsistent responses undermine the "validity" of respondents replies. But how can people respond consistently in a complex social order that is itself rent by contradictory expectations?".

Indeed, in this respect we may be wise to accept Keesing's words of caution (1987:383). We must be wary of attributing a more global or coherent model to our subjects than they themselves cognize. Contradiction is built into these models; it is not a weakness of the tools for uncovering the models themselves. If this point is indeed true, then it may well be that the essence of military organization is based on paradox or contradiction. Thus the internally contradictory image of a "thinking automaton" captures a combination of qualities that characterize soldiers. In the same vein, the picture of highly inspired but emotionally restrained individuals captures the motivational combination distinguishing Israeli troops.

NOTES

1. A logical analysis of such models "often reveals them to be fairly inconsistent in the sense that antonymous presuppositions are simultaneously held by people who may be unaware of, or simply not concerned by, contradiction. Indeed, this concern with internal consistency may be particular to Western cultures, which appear most obsessed with balance and dissonance, compared with non-Western cultures" (Furnham 1987: 208).

Epilogue:
My Israeli Military:
A Disappearing World?

❧❧❧

*I*t may now be appropriate to return to an examination of the relationship between this volume and what may be termed its specific historical context. It may be pertinent because such an exploration touches upon the links between anthropology (or more generally the human sciences) and studies of the military, and the place of my specific inquiry in the interrogation of war and national service in Israeli society.

A number of scholars have noted that while anthropologists often have studied aspects of conflict among tribal or agricultural societies, they scarcely have examined the place of the military and of war in complex industrialized societies (Goldschmidt 1989: 9; Mandelbaum 1989). Greenhouse (1989: 49) suggests that because of the common premise pervading our discipline that war is pathological and a professional value orientation that opposes armed aggression, key cultural questions about conflict and the armed forces have been obscured.[1] I would add that the essentially distrustful attitude to political authorities that characterizes most professional (Western) anthropologists, has been intensified by the legacy of the Vietnam War, which still is habitually seen as an essentially corrupt undertaking.

But what kinds of "cultural" questions can anthropologists ask about such matters as armed conflicts? In what is still very much an exceptional ethnography of Vietnam veterans, Greenhouse suggests that

[o]bedience is not necessarily a decision made in terms of national interest versus self-interest, life versus death, but [may] be the consequence of a different sort of cultural process. That process involves the formation of propositions that positively connect the state, the law, and the individual, including the acceptance of military service. For these reasons, the agenda for anthropology in questions of war and peace is not only in gaining an understanding of the *decision* to fight, but of the sociocultural logic that simultaneously requires and obviates the decision (1989: 50–51 emphasis in original).

Consequently, what Greenhouse suggests is that we look at the assumptions underlying discussions about, and the actions of, the armed forces. She found that the striking element in her research on American soldiers was

that the ideals that create harmony at the local level – discipline and faith – are exactly the same ones that bring soldiers to war. In other words, there is something in the American conception of order that cancels the opposition between peace and war; peace and war are on the same side of a larger opposition between order and disorder (Greenhouse 1989: 58).

In Israel, slightly different ideals work to induce soldiers to commit themselves to military service. Let me explicate these ideals through an examination of my own personal journey to reflection.

In the preface, I explained that this volume began with my attempt to make sense of my experience, and the experiences of my fellow soldiers, during the Intifada. My initial work culminated in "Masks and Soldiering: The Israeli Army and the Palestinian Uprising" (Ben-Ari 1989). In that article, my contention was that despite the circumstances of the Intifada, which necessitated police-like activities, the military ethos soon drew soldiers and officers to define their role through an essentially military orientation. I found that the Intifada was not interpreted as a unique case of civilians undertaking an uprising for national liberation, but rather was defined as "just" another military mission (essentially, like the missions carried out in any "regular" war against regular armies). This happened, I maintained, through a process of "naturalization" that worked through the organizational structure and rules of the battalion. I tried to explain the crucial role of the unit's reality constructors – the officers and senior NCOs – in providing the men of the unit with answers to questions about "who are we?" and "what are we doing here?" But as Paine (1992), commenting on my article, perceptively noted, my analysis raised much wider questions. As I showed, the soldiers (and myself very much included) had an *a priori* text, actualized in organizational roles, small groups, and dictates, which channelled our perception of conflict and the enemy in the Intifada. What was significant in this process was that this military text was also a Zionist text.

Many members of my unit, including myself, belong to Israel's "liberal, enlightened, Western-oriented" citizens: to a group self-styled as "Zionism with a conscience" (Cohen 1988). But we could not engage in a truly reflective examination of the situation. By defining periods of service during the Intifada as periods of military duty (as opposed to police actions to control civilians) the soldiers (and, again, myself among them) related their personal understanding to the grand narrative of the IDF protecting the very survival of the nation-state. In this manner, the Palestinian Uprising was "naturalized" not only by relating it to the combat schema, but no less importantly by allowing its subordination to the *a priori* Zionist text. In other words, in comprehending the Intifada as a "normal" or "natural" military situation, the activities of the unit were linked to the notion that military actions by Israeli soldiers are ultimately related to the safety and security of the country. To paraphrase Paine, it can be suggested that much in Israeli culture can be understood in just those terms: the need to defend the validity of what has been done (the establishment and defense of a Jewish state) at the expense of a deeper reflection (1992: 191–2).

While Paine underscores the existence of a ready-made text used to interpret military activities of the IDF, my analysis illuminates the actual processes by which this deeper reflection was avoided, was deflected.[2] Talk about soldiers-as-machines, discussions about the reactive capacities of units and commanders, and commentary about emotional control in the service of military missions are all reflective in one sense: they are occasions during which troops contemplate their actions. But because such debates are essentially considerations of practical matters (tactics, logistics, or drills, for example) they defer reflection about the aims of wars or of military service, and about the very necessity of military force. In the IDF, discussions in and around the term *miktso'anut* (professionalism) encapsulate this process. Based on the combat schema, this term is a sort of shorthand expression containing the criteria by which soldiers and commanders are appraised. But because deliberations about *miktso'anut* take place within relatively cohesive small groups and strong ties to commanders, and because they reverberate with notions of masculinity, they tend to divert troops from a deeper contemplation of military missions.

To put this point picturesquely, because self-reflection in the army is habitually and systematically channelled toward making humans fit the requirements of a mechanical organization there is little necessity for reflecting about the place of the military machine in the wider environment. In other words, deliberation about military means often implies that a deeper reflexivity is denied.[3]

Take for example, the notion of enemy civilians. As I showed in Chapter 6, using "undue force" – that is, hitting, pushing, beating, or shooting – against civilians is considered an aberration in many units of the IDF. It is an aberration not just because of the basic humanity or human values desired of the soldiers. No less importantly, these are aberrations because they indicate a lack of professionalism. Using "undue force," to reiterate, is viewed as a lack of control and an inability to master oneself and the situation. Conversely, soldiers who cannot control themselves and commanders who cannot control their troops (and themselves) are considered to be inept or nonprofessional. In the logic of the machine metaphor, these men are labelled as "ill-fitting" or "mal-functioning" parts of the unit. Thus all a commander has to do is to replace these "mechanical parts" so that the battalion can continue to perform. Theoretically speaking, cognitive models like the combat schema are more than meanings that obfuscate; their power lies in providing a template from which meanings are actively derived.

Why have I turned reflective? To be sure, it "is generally the case that the powerful have little reason to reflect on their position as normal, just, or inevitable" (Morgan 1992: 30). This situation is true whether we are thinking of class, ethnicity, gender, or national affiliation. But in times of crisis at least some members of a society's dominant categories are forced to consider anew their position in society. Israel has been undergoing a set or processes in the past two-and-a-half decades that have forced (or allowed) public reflection about the military and armed conflict. More specifically, the connection between the focus of my study and present historical circumstances is related to political, social, demographic and economic changes that since 1967 have transformed the country's prevailing political cultures and sentiments (see Aronoff 1989; Horowitz and Lissak 1989; Lustick 1988). Some of the more important of these changes are these: a greater acceptance of the Jewish Diaspora and the concomitant openness to *Jewish* "ethnic pluralism"; a certain enhancement of religious sentiments and a related strengthening of nationalistic feelings among major segments of society; a changed attitude toward the Holocaust and a greater willingness to search for continuities with past Jewish identities; the eruption of the Intifada and the increased militancy of Israeli-Arabs and the uneasiness this has generated among many Israeli-Jews; and, following Israel's debacle in Lebanon, the decreased legitimacy of such institutions as the army (Ben-Ari and Bilu 1997). Indeed, "After the Lebanon War and during its later phases, no holds were barred. The holiest cows were slaughtered, the very basic concept of the rightness and moral code of the IDF was no longer a clear, unquestioned tenet" (Shalit 1988: 173).

Today, we find continued challenges and questioning of previously undisputed assumptions held by state authorities and the majority of the population about military qualities and behavior. Despite the hardline taken by many of Israel's governments, many groups in contemporary Israeli society are no longer willing to grant the IDF its previous status of unquestioned professionalism and to view "state security" consider-ations as the only (or primary) criteria for national decision making. We now witness signs of dissent about such matters as the role of women in the army and in combat, the links between families and military author-ities, the official reasons for, and handling of, suicides, or the symbolism of graves and military memorials. Thus my volume should be seen as part of a much wider interrogation of war and the military that is now taking place in Israeli society. The contribution of my volume to this trend lies in providing a detailed, empirically based, account of the rela-tion between images of enemies, conflict, motivation, and emotional control. But paradoxically, it is precisely the changed historical context that has allowed me to write this book, which both reflects and is an out-come of these social circumstances.

At this historical moment, the Israeli government has signed peace accords with Egypt and Jordan, and talks are continuing with represen-tatives of the Palestinian state as well as with officials of the Syrian regime. If these processes will carry on, are the Israeli armed forces – at least as we now know them —going to disappear? Such questions imply issues related to the armed forces in general and the IDF in particular. Am I writing about an anthropological relic? Is my ethnography little more than an exercise in "salvage anthropology," a means to document a vanishing world?

As I suggested in the Introduction, despite the advent of various technological innovations it will probably remain true militarily that only ground troops can take and hold land. Moreover, among these troops, the infantry will continue to epitomize the prototypical pattern of face-to-face combat against antagonists. In this sense my kind of analysis will continue to be of relevance to the study of the military. Even given the tendency of Middle Eastern politics to change and to be unpredictable and the tendency of some Israeli governments to perpetuate the combined image (and reality) of nationhood and military power, the peace processes will probably (and hopefully) continue. This will imply that in the very long run, the ground forces of the IDF may be transformed in terms of modes of thinking, behavior, and organizational arrangements. However, if one reads this volume not only as a study of a specific kind of unit (or only of the military as an organization) but also as an interrogation of the dominant sectors of Israeli society, then it contributes toward a greater awareness of the contours and limits of this dominant position.

NOTES

1. Indeed, the "fact is that war is not always and not only an accident or a function of sociocultural breakdown in international relations. Warfare and the ability to mobilize for war can be signs that in the eyes of its members, society works, that its social order is viable" (Greenhouse 1989: 49).
2. I am indebted to Efrat Ben-Ze'ev for helping me to clarify this point.
3. In a related vein, as Helman observes, in participating in different military activities (patrolling, guarding, or training, for example) the individual is reproducing the overall "logic" of the state and the centrality of "security" as its organizing principle (1993: 158 ff.).

Appendix I:
Fieldwork and the
Ethnographic Approach

୶ଡ଼୶ଡ଼ଡ଼

*A*ny piece of social research should spell out its methodological tools in a way that enables readers to appraise their appropriateness. In other words, I think it important to describe as clearly as possible the research procedures that I used so that the limits and benefits of my interpretations may be evaluated. In this appendix I describe and explain my field methods while in Appendix II I examine the procedures I used in analyzing my data. This depiction will explain the foundations of the ethnographic approach and provide an idea of the kinds of data on which my contentions are based.

Gathering Data

Throughout the years of fieldwork, I utilized stints in the army, and occasionally other periods, to gather information based on participation, observation, and interviews. In my official capacity as adjutant I attended all staff, summing-up, personnel, and planning meetings. I often accompanied (commonly acting as driver) the battalion's commander, his deputy, or other staff officers during their visits, tours, and patrols of places where the battalion's men were training or being deployed. When I talked to company clerks about personnel matters, our discussions frequently branched off into examinations of the informal dynamics of army units. Almost invariably, I was invited for the ubiquitous coffee sessions that I mentioned before, and other times I visited people on guard duty for a chat or a look at the scenery. During live-fire exercises (I had a very small role to play in these maneuvers), I walked around with a little notebook or a tape recorder and entered observations about things that interested me.

I always tried to be clear that my purpose in collecting material was for a book about the unit, and I gave copies of the Hebrew version of my paper on the Intifada (Ben-Ari 1989) to whomever was interested. After a while, and especially after a number of officers and soldiers had read this article, people would initiate discussions with me about my project and tell me the latest battalion jokes. (They knew that I had made a habit of collecting gags and quips related to military life.) Although a few fellow officers sometimes made fun at how I was furthering my academic career by turning them into informants, I never encountered any resistance or even a hint of criticism about my intention of doing research on military life. Other soldiers (perhaps unfamiliar with the aims of social science) thought that I was writing a history of the unit, as this was the battalion that held some of the outposts on the Suez Canal at the beginning of the Yom Kippur War in 1973. As I found when doing fieldwork elsewhere, some men found it amazing that I was interested in writing about their everyday, mundane lives as reserve troops.

An interesting source of information about "collective" self-analysis were the long trips to and from Jerusalem (my home) with other soldiers, NCOs, and officers. As in any closely knit organization, these two- to four-hour trips in which three or four of us were ensconced in the relative privacy of cars provided opportunities to report, analyze, and evaluate what was going on in the unit. Trips on the first day going to reserve duty always seemed to be occasions for us to begin to take on our military persona by talking of military matters; journeys back home provided chances to sum up a particular stint and to start winding down toward civilian life.

I carried out about thirty interviews during fieldwork. While the term "interview" grants these occasions an air of structured engagements, and while I did go through an ordered set of questions, in reality they were often conversations. In holding these exchanges, I tried to get as wide a view as possible of the unit; thus they were held with the battalion's commanders, NCOs, soldiers from all five companies, medics, two drivers, two clerks, and a cook. I felt that interviews with "ordinary" soldiers were especially important in order to get out of an overly "officer-centric" view of things. In this endeavor I was aided both by my formal capacity and by my fieldwork persona. As the officer in charge of personnel, I likened part of my job to that of a social worker with whom it is legitimate to air one's grievances, or to talk about a variety of problematic matters. My persona, a bit of a "softy" and a scholar study-ing something vaguely related to psychology, probably helped in getting people to open up as well. While I have no comparative data to back this point up, it is my impression that I was helped in my research by the relative egalitarianism of the IDF, a factor that allows for considerable openness between ranks.

I was aided throughout my research by one of the most characteristic qualities of military life: boredom. I often felt that soldiers regarded talks with me as a good way to pass the time. Frequently, after it was known that I "was writing a book," my mere presence would prompt people to talk of the military or of their lives. In this regard, however, I repeatedly sensed that I was lending an attentive ear to people's ongoing interests rather than having them answer questions that arose out of my own research agenda. Privacy is a rare commodity in the army; thus the inter-views were often held in relatively private spaces like the commander's office (when he was away), synagogue, infirmary, or private cars. Topics ranged from past career or motivation for serving and promotion, to more intimate things like fear in combat, going AWOL, or attitudes to the Intifada.

The data itself – not unlike my findings in other research projects – were recorded in a journal and entered chronologically. As far as possible, I took time off from my regular duties either to write full-scale descrip-tions of activities, or to jot down at least elementary scratch notes that I expanded every few days. My fieldwork journal now includes observa-tions, long and short parts of conversations, unclassified documents (invitations to parties or letters from commanders, for example), and some very rudimentary thoughts about analysis. In addition, all the interviews were taped and later transcribed by a research assistant into the field journal.

The Ethnographic Approach

Why use the ethnographic, or what is called in sociology the naturalistic, approach? Methodologically speaking, this approach provides the kind of rich data needed for examining social knowledge and meaning systems (Orum et al. 1991:12). It can provide such data because it focuses on the concrete activities undertaken by people – like discussions, conversations, or story-telling – rather than directly on complex notions, beliefs, or folk models. Such an approach allows us to focus on the explicit images, metaphors, or reasonings through which more abstract notions are expressed. The qualitative approach is especially useful for gathering data on "natural" language use in a way that comes as close as possible to the understandings of the participants of their own actions. Finally, such a focus enables one to show how meanings are related to the dynamics of the social world. They are related because people use such images to carry out a host of pragmatic tasks such as evaluating, characterizing, or prescribing.

In this sense gathering data at the level of a battalion has some distinct advantages. On the one hand it is probably the largest unit within which I could have known everyone by face if not by name. On the other hand, the diversity it encompasses – the different kinds of companies and the array of roles – allowed me to investigate the extent to which meanings are shared across the battalion's constituent units and various military roles. Thus in contrast to research carried out on the level of a rifle company, data gathered at this level allowed me to obtain not only the perspectives of "regular" infantry soldiers and lower echelon officers, but also the views of more senior commanders, staff and administrative officers, noncombat support soldiers, or specialist troops dealing with such matters as communications or intelligence.

To what extent did the men "level" with me? This question bears methodological implications for any study purporting to examine meaning. First, I would argue that openness and honesty marked my interactions simply because one cannot hide feelings, actions, and (frequently) thoughts while on reserve duty; one is in the public gaze for many days and weeks. Second, I think that people like to talk, and even in regard to intimate topics, once a modicum of trust has been built up in interviews or conversations people are willing to explore painful or difficult matters. Even a short list of the difficulties discussed with me would seem to indicate a relatively high level of candor: hatred of senior NCOs, resentment of being exploited, disappointment at not being promoted, fear of parachuting, sense of personal responsibility for casualties during exercises, as well as problems associated with civilian life (worries about being unemployed, financial predicaments, or health problems of relatives, for instance). Paradoxically, it may well be that it is precisely during stints of army service – that is, away from the "usual" limits of civilian life and within a different set of constraints – that it may be possible for men to be more truthful about these matters.

A closely related methodological matter has to do with the intrusion of the anthropologist into the life of the people being researched. Here the problem is the extent to which the unit's men standardized their answers or views because of my presence or prodding. In this regard, I would argue that "natives" tend to standardize their acts, utterances, and other manners of expression whether "we" scholars are there or not. Stories, talk, metaphors, or ways of thinking have a great coercive power that overrides external influences including the ethnographer (Peacock 1986:70). Thus I probably did add a greater awareness, a measure of self-examination to the men of the battalion, but I do not think that I altered things. It would be a measure of little more than self-delusion or self-aggrandizement to think that the unit changed in some fundamental way because of my presence or my research.

In a similar vein, some people may be more inclined to introspection or trained to self-examination (or both) and thus be able to provide a more coherent view of the meaning guiding their lives than others. In most cases the men in my unit – barring a few exceptions – were unlike "professional complicators" (Geertz 1983: 89) such as priests, poets, intellectuals, or social scientists (like me) whose business it is to reflect and contemplate. By the same token again, some situations may be more conducive to self-examination: interviews, private meetings, or musings for instance. As an anthropologist I tried to be aware of the peculiarity of such people and situations in reconstructing the folk knowledge of the culture I studied.

Is my membership in the unit not a sign of methodological weakness? Like the social role of any researcher, my position presents both strengths and weaknesses. I assume, of course, that no perfectly objective knowledge of a situation is possible; knowledge is always relative to the knower (see Peacock 1986: 110). The major disadvantages of my approach, it may be argued, are the biases and lack of proper "distance" from the unit and its dynamics. Throughout the text, I have tried as much as possible to be clear about my prejudices and preferences, and to explicitly state the limits of my assertions. On the reverse side, the major advantages of my participation in the unit are twofold: first, in my being close to the way the folk models and meanings are actualized in the reality of the unit; and second in my ability to use my native understandings of soldiering and of commanding in themselves as a resource.

Ultimately, the strengths and weaknesses of my work are predicated on my ability to achieve what interpretive social scientists call a reflexive stance towards the unit and towards the meaning of soldiering. By this notion is meant first of all, an ongoing effort not to rely only on introspection, but to meticulously record, describe, analyze and eventually formulate my findings in a way that will allow them to be critiqued by others. This notion also implies that I continuously verify my native understandings with other sources and frame my interpretations in ways that will allow a confrontation between them and other assertions found in the literature on the military.

Stated succinctly, the kind of research I carried out raises the issue of finding the "right" distance from one's own society in order to be able to study it. In this sense, it may well be worthwhile for British and American readers to remember that Israeli anthropology, like the anthropology of mainland Europe (Lofgren 1987), has had a need to devise techniques, not so much for getting into a new culture, as for getting out of all too familiar surroundings. These techniques seem to be especially important for the study of matters that touch upon some very basic (and emotionally loaded) issues such as military identity, assumptions about conflict, and images of enemies.

What methods and procedures did I use in order to achieve this distancing, the rephrasing and reframing of my personal experience? One approach that has always been part of the anthropological armature has been the study of language. Along these lines, I realized early on that an inspection of the language used in the Israeli military may uncover some of the meanings attached to military service. For example, the translation of army phrases and terms into English prompted me to scrutinize the connotations of these expressions in Hebrew. In this respect, the IDF (like all armies) has its own rather specialized language ranging from formal and semiformal jargon and acronyms to vernacular idioms and slang. Throughout my research I consistently encountered reminders of just how specialized this military argot is. While I am usually fully bilingual and switch effortlessly between Hebrew and English, I found myself making extensive use of Hebrew-English and English military dictionaries (Burla 1988; Shafritz, Shafritz and Robertson 1989) whenever I wrote or tried to explain my research to non-Israelis. There were many terms that I could easily use in Hebrew but just did not know in English: for instance, "armored personnel carrier", "combat readiness," "operational deployment" as well as *ben-zona* (son of a bitch), or *frier* (sucker). The translation of terms into English required a special effort for it was (like much of anthropological exegesis) not only a matter of technical conversion, but also an awareness of the distinctive cultural connotations of these terms.

Another method of distancing had to do with deliberate attempts at defamiliarizing my material, at making my field data alien (Marcus and Fischer 1986). The primary manner by which I carried out this exercise was by relating my material to a variety of theoretical formulations elicited in other contexts. For example, I linked my data to explanations of small group formation in the American army in Korea and Vietnam and (yes) to the Wehrmacht in the Second World War, to concepts drawn from the analysis of metaphors in Mediterranean cultures, to analytical tools taken from feminism in regard to emotional control among policemen and policewomen, or to new suggestions found in the social scientific study of embodiment and of emotions. All of these operations forced me to reflect about my data from a more detached vantage point.

Appendix II:
Notes on the Methodology
of Interpretation

I devoted the previous appendix to my fieldwork, that is, the processes of gathering material. In this methodological supplement let me spell out the procedures I used in order to make sense of my data during the stages of interpretation (analysis and writing).

Reliability usually means the ability to replicate the original study using the same research instrument to obtain the same results. Much qualitative work is said to be difficult because there is a lack of standardization. Each social scientist, as it were, is said to write his or her own story, and there is little to guarantee that several social scientists will report the same story. In this sense, my approach is probably not replicable. On the other hand this does not preclude the possibility that I report my findings and my methods in a way that can be appraised by other scholars.

Our understandings of the world are founded on many tacit assumptions, assumptions that are often transparent to us (Quinn and Holland 1987:14). Once learned, this tacit knowledge becomes what one sees with but seldom what one sees. Technically this quality of folk knowledge is termed referential transparency, which means knowledge which is used but is usually left unquestioned by its bearer. Geertz (1983:87) terms this quality of common sense knowledge, the "of-courseness" of things. Hence the methodological problem: how, and on the basis of what evidence, does one reconstruct the mental models people use but do not often explicitly reflect upon or articulate? We need a method that will aid us in uncovering the manner by which such naturally occurring tasks as categorizing, reasoning, remembering, or problem solving are done. Thus, for example, it is not enough to know what "*kor ruach*" is; one must understand how it is used by soldiers to make sense of military life.

I begin with a rather concrete description of my work in order to answer this question. I began to analyze my data by making two initial reviews of all my fieldnotes and categorizing the data into a number of general categories. I then decided to focus on a few key interviews that seemed to me to be especially revelatory either because they were held with more introspective informants who were capable of formulating their thoughts, or because they seemed to be "rich" in terms of the understandings which could be gleaned from them. Next, going over these five or six interviews I made lists of the metaphors the men used. I then began to see that these metaphors all divided along the lines of what I later understood to be the machine and brain metaphors and the rhetoric of emotional control.

At the same time I systematically reviewed some general studies of the armed forces and of the IDF and a number of works in cognitive anthropology. During the next stage I looked for a schema or scenario that could pull these diverse metaphors together and arrived upon the combat and motivation schemas. Finally, after writing a draft of my thesis, I returned to my fieldnotes to check whether my understanding was supported or not by other data. Here I especially looked for data elicited in contexts other than formal interviews (observations, casual remarks, or meetings, for instance). I also went back to the variety of secondary sources about the IDF and other military establishments for the same reasons.

The manner in which I proceeded was a sort of circle of activities – in the social sciences this is called the hermeneutic circle – that involved a movement between data, theory, provisional interpretation, data, theory, and reinterpretation. This kind of intellectual movement (Geertz 1983:69) is a sort of continuous dialectic between the most local detail and the most global structure, between the brief phrase a soldier had used and my more general model of what he is talking about. The movement is based on bringing the local detail and the global structure into a sort of simultaneous view so that each may explicate the other.

Within this movement of analysis and corroboration I used two kinds of approaches. First, I explicitly utilized my own native speaker's knowledge; second, I carefully tested this knowledge in terms of independent observations within my unit and from the scholarly literature on the military. For example, I used introspection, that is my own intuitions as a native speaker of Hebrew and as a member of the battalion, as a starting point for examining such concepts as "*kor ruach*," or "*lachatz*," but then I analyzed how these terms (or their synonyms) were used in the natural discourse as it occurred in various contexts in the battalion. At other times I looked at other types of discourse – e.g. a narrative or story about the Lebanon war – in order to understand what the narrator highlighted or elaborated, or left unsaid. The point underlying all of these efforts was to come as close as possible to the way the men themselves make use of their folk knowledge. Thus in regard to validity, my kind of research has clear advantages because it permits me to assemble complementary and overlapping measures or indicators of the same phenomenon. This is what Denzin (1978) calls the triangulation of sources. Indeed, anthropologists, like many qualitatively minded scholars, try to maximize validity, and to an extent reliability, through the use of an eclectic mix of research operations (Pelto and Pelto 1970:34).

APPENDIX III:
FOLK AND SCIENTIFIC MODELS

With the popularization of science and with the spread of mass higher education, it is not surprising that scientific models are incorporated into the models people use in their everyday lives. For example, the men of the unit borrow social scientific terms to talk about such things as need-fulfillment, risk-seeking, or the links between workplace atmosphere and job satisfaction. But this borrowing is selective, because popular versions tend to use only a small number of (often isolated) concepts taken from scientific models. Hence in talking of need-fulfillment, the men do not devise a hierarchy of needs, nor are they explicit about the way needs can be fulfilled in different contexts. Moreover, unlike scientific theories, "folk" models are unlikely to be tested systematically, or to be stated in terms of clear lines of causality and isolation of variables. They are nevertheless theories of behavior.

In addition, unlike many scientific theories, folk models are used not only to describe, explain, or analyze, but are also used to evaluate, prescribe, and label. Here I do not deny that scientific theories carry their own biases and valuations, nor that common sense knowledge can be developed, questioned, formalized, or contemplated (Geertz 1983:76). I simply propose that in the realm of folk knowledge, the normative dimension is much more explicit. Because of the taken-for-granted quality of folk models there is usually much less structured reflectivity about their internal organization and consistency, or indeed about the normative assumptions which undergird them.

Finally, a word about the explicitness of the models should be said. Some knowledge is probably more habitual and easily put into words than other knowledge. To put this point another way, some knowledge is under conscious and voluntary control while other knowledge is less available for introspection and articulation. Thus for example, it is my impression that for the men of the unit, the combat schema is more easily formulated than the rhetoric of emotional control that underlies it. Moreover, most informants may not even have an organized view of the entire model. They may use the model but cannot produce a reasonable description of it. In this sense, the knowledge of folk models is like a well learned set of procedures one knows in order to carry out tasks (like riding a bicycle) rather than a body of facts that one can recount (like a geography or history of some state) (D'Andrade 1987:114; D'Andrade 1995:172). For example, while all of the men of the unit use the model of combat in evaluating military situations, they rarely if ever formulate their thinking in the same systematic manner by which Gal (1988) has set out the parameters of a professional psychological model of stress in combat.

BIBLIOGRAPHY

Abu-Lughod, Lila, and Catherine A. Lutz. 1990."Introduction: Emotion, Discourse, and the Politics of Everyday Life," in Catherine A. Lutz and Lila Abu-Lughod (eds.). *Language and the Politics of Emotion.* Cambridge: Cambridge University Press.

Amir, Yehuda. 1969. "The Effectiveness of the Kibbutz-Born Soldier in the Israel Defence Forces." *Human Relations* 22(4): 333-44.

Aronoff, Myron. 1989. *Israeli Visions and Divisions: Cultural Change and Political Conflict.* New Brunswick, N.J.: Transaction.

Aronoff, Myron. 1993. "The Origins of Israeli Political Culture," in Ehud Sprinzak and Larry Diamond (eds.). *Israeli Democracy Under Stress.* Boulder: Lynne Rienner.

Bailey, F.G. 1983. *The Tactical Uses of Passion.* Ithaca: Cornell University Press.

Ballard, John A., and Aliecia J. McDowell. 1991. "Hate and Combat Behavior." *Armed Forces and Society* 17(2): 229–41.

Bar-Kochva, Moshe (Bril). 1989. *Chariots of Steel.* Tel Aviv: Ministry of Defence. (Hebrew)

Ben-Ari, Eyal. 1989. "Masks and Soldiering: The Israeli Army and the Palestinian Uprising." *Cultural Anthropology* 4(4): 372–89.

Ben-Ari, Eyal, and Yoram Bilu, eds. 1997. *Grasping Land: Space and Place in Contemporary Israeli Discourse and Experience.* Albany: State University of New York Press.

Ben-Ari, Eyal and Edna Lomsky-Feder. Forthcoming. "Introductory Essay: Cultural Constructions of War and the Military in Israel," in Edna Lomsky-Feder and Eyal Ben-Ari (eds.). *The Military and Militarism in Israeli Society.* Albany: State University of New York Press.

Ben-Eliezer, Uri. 1995a. *The Emergence of Israeli Militarism, 1936–1956.* Tel Aviv: Dvir. (Hebrew)

—— 1995b. "A Nation-in-Arms: State, Nation, and Militarism in Israel's First Years." *Comparative Studies in Society and History* 37(2): 264–85.

Boene, Bernard. 1990. "How Unique Should the Military Be? A Review of Representative Literature and Outline of Synthetic Formulation." *European Journal of Sociology* 31(1): 3–59.

Bourdieu, Pierre. 1977. *Outline of a Theory of Practice*. Cambridge: Cambridge University Press.

Brandes, Stanley. 1980. *Metaphors of Masculinity: Sex and Status in Andalusian Folklore*. Philadelphia: University of Pennsylvania Press.

Breznitz, S., ed. 1983. *Stress in Israel*. New York: Van Nostrand.

Bruner, Edward M., and Phyllis Gorfain. 1983. "Dialogic Narration and the Paradoxes of Masada," in Edward M. Bruner (ed.): *Text, Play and Story*. Washington D.C.: Proceedings of the American Ethnological Society.

Buck, James H., and Lawrence Korb, eds. 1981. *Military Leadership*. Beverly Hills: Sage.

Cameron, Craig M. 1994. *American Samurai: Myth, Imagination, and the Conduct of Battle in the First Marine Division, 1941–1951*. Cambridge: Cambridge University Press.

Clark, M. Margaret. 1989. "The Cultural Patterning of Risk-Seeking Behavior: Implications for Armed Conflict," in Mary LeCron Foster and Robert A. Rubinstein (eds.). *Peace and War: Cross-Cultural Perspectives*. New Brunswick: Transaction.

Cohen, Stanley. 1988. "Criminology and the Uprising." *Tikkun* 3(5): 60–52, 95–96.

Cohen, Stuart. 1995. "The Israeli Defense Forces (IDF): From a 'People's Army' to a 'Professional Military' – Causes and Implications." *Armed Forces and Society* 21(2): 237–54.

Csiksentmihalyi, Mihaly. 1975. *Beyond Boredom and Anxiety*. San Francisco: Jossey-Bass.

Dandeker, C. 1992. "The Bureaucratization of Force," in Lawrence Freedman (ed.). *War*. Oxford: Oxford University Press.

D'Andrade, Roy. 1987. "A Folk Model of the Mind," in Dorothy Holland and Naomi Quinn (eds.). *Cultural Models in Language and Thought*. Cambridge: Cambridge University Press.

—— 1992. "Schemas and Motivation," in Roy G. D'Andrade and Claudia Strauss (eds.). *Human Motives and Cultural Models*. Cambridge: Cambridge University Press.

—— 1995. *The Development of Cognitive Anthropology*. Cambridge: Cambridge University Press.

Denzin, Norman K. 1978. *The Research Act: A Theoretical Introduction to Sociological Methods*. New York: McGraw-Hill.

Dominguez, Virginia R. 1989. "The Politics of Heritage in Contemporary Israel." *American Ethnological Monograph Series*, Number 2: 130–47.

Dower, John W. 1986. *War Without Mercy: Race and Power in the Pacific War.* New York: Pantheon.

Dunivin, Karen O. 1994. "Military Culture: Change and Continuity." *Armed Forces and Society* 20(4): 531–47.

Dyer, Gwynne. 1985. *War.* New York: Crown Publishers.

Ehrlich, Avishai. 1987. "Israel: Conflict, War and Social Change," in Colin Creighton and Martin Shaw (eds.). *The Sociology of War and Peace.* London: Macmillan.

Eisenhart, R. Wayne. 1975. "You Can't Hack It Little Girl: A Discussion of the Covert Psychological Agenda of Modern Combat Training." *Journal of Social Issues* 31(4): 13–23.

Eitan, Rephael (Raful), with Dov Goldstein. 1985. *The Story of a Soldier.* Tel Aviv: Ma'ariv. (Hebrew)

Eldar, Mike. 1993. *Flotilla 13: The Story of Israel's Naval Commandos.* Tel Aviv: Ma'ariv. (Hebrew)

Feige, Michael, and Eyal Ben-Ari. 1991. "Card Games and an Israeli Army Unit: An Interpretive Case Study." *Armed Forces and Society* 17(3): 439–48.

Feld, Maury D. 1977. *The Structure of Violence: Armed Forces as Social Systems.* Beverly Hills: Sage.

Fernandez, James. 1986. *Persuasions and Performances: The Play of Tropes in Culture.* Indiana: Indiana University Press.

Frank, Jerome D. 1989. "Sociopsychological Aspects of the Prevention of Nuclear War," in Mary Lecron Foster and Robert A. Rubinstein (eds.): *Peace and War: Cross-Cultural Perspectives.* New Brunswick: Transaction.

Furnham, Adrian. 1987. *Lay Theories: Everyday Understanding of Problems in the Social Sciences.* Oxford: Pergamon.

Fussel, Paul. 1975. *The Great War and Modern Memory.* New York: Oxford University Press.

—— 1989. *Wartime: Understanding and Behavior in the Second World War.* New York: Oxford University Press.

Gabriel, Richard A. 1984. *Operation Peace for Galilee.* New York: Hill and Wang.

—— 1987. *No More Heroes: Madness & Psychiatry in War.* New York: Hill and Wang.

Gal, Michael. 1973. "The Scouting Unit as a Social Group." *Shdemot* 40: 34–50. (Hebrew)

Gal, Reuven. 1986. *A Portrait of the Israeli Soldier.* New York: Greenwood Press.

—— 1988. *Stressful Combat Situations: Causes, Reactions and Coping.* Zichron Ya'akov: The Israel Institute for Military Studies.

Gal, Reuven, ed. 1990. *The Seventh War: The Effects of the Intifada on the Israeli Society.* Tel Aviv: Hakibbutz Hameuchad. (Hebrew)

Gal-Or, Naomi. 1988. "The IDF and the Unconventional War or the Palestinian Factor and the National Security Doctrine of Israel," *international Problems* 50(1–2): 20–33. (Hebrew)

Geertz, Clifford. 1983. *Local Knowledge: Further Essays in Interpretive Anthropology.* New York: Basic Books.

Giddens, Anthony. 1985. *The Nation-State and Violence.* Cambridge: Polity.

Gilmore, David D. 1990. *Manhood in the Making: Cultural Concepts of Masculinity.* New Haven: Yale University Press.

Goldberg-Weil, Na'ama. 1996. "Differences in Leadership Patterns Between the Infantry and Armored Corps at the Level of Company Commanders." Masters thesis, The Hebrew University of Jerusalem.

Goldschmidt, Walter. 1989. "Personal Motivation and Institutionalized Conflict," in Mary LeCron Foster and Robert A. Rubinstein (eds.). *Peace and War: Cross-Cultural Perspectives.* New Brunswick: Transaction.

Greenbaum, Charles W. 1979. "The Small Group Under the Gun: Uses of Small Groups in Battle Conditions." *Journal of Applied Behavioral Science* 15: 392–405.

Greenhouse, Carol J. 1989. "Fighting For Peace," in Mary LeCron Foster and Robert A. Rubinstein (eds.). *Peace and War: Cross-Cultural Perspectives.* New Brunswick: Transaction.

Grossman, Dave. 1995. *On Killing: The Psychological Cost of Learning to Kill in War and Society.* Boston: Little Brown.

Handelman, Don, and Elihu Katz. 1995. "State Ceremonies of Israel: Remembrance Day and Independence Day," in Shlomo Deshen, Charles Liebman and Moshe Shokeid (eds.). *Israeli Judaism: The Sociology of Religion in Israel.* New Brunswick, N.J.: Transaction.

Handelman, Don, and Lea Shamgar-Handelman. 1997. "The Presence of Absence: The Memorialization of National Death in Israel," in Eyal Ben-Ari and Yoram Bilu (eds.). *Grasping Land: Space and Place in Contemporary Israeli Discourse and Experience.* Albany: State University of New York Press.

Harries-Jenkins, Gwyn. 1986. "Role Images, Military Attitudes, and Enlisted Culture in Great Britain," in David R. Segal and H. Wallace Sinaiko (eds.): *Life in the Rank and File.* Washington D.C.: Pergamon-Brassy's.

Harries-Jenkins, Gwyn and Charles C. Moskos. 1981. "Trend Report: Armed Forces and Society." *Current Sociology* 29(3): 1–43.

Hasdai, Yaakov. 1982. "'Doers' and 'Thinkers' in the IDF." *The Jerusalem Quarterly* 24: 13–25.

Haste, Helen. 1993. *The Sexual Metaphor.* New York: Harvester/Wheatsheaf.

Helman, Sarit. 1992. "Paradigmatic War Rationality and the Constitution of the "Different" Rationality of the Lebanon War." The Hebrew University: Department of Sociology and Anthropology.

Helman, Sarit. 1993. "Conscientious Objection to Military Service as an Attempt to Redefine the Content of Citizenship." Ph.D Diss., The Hebrew University of Jerusalem.

Holland, Dorothy, and Debra Skinner. 1987. "Prestige and Intimacy: The Cultural Models Behind American's Talk about Gender," in Dorothy

Holland and Naomi Quinn (eds.). *Cultural Models in Language and Thought.* Cambridge: Cambridge University Press.

Holmes, Richard. 1985. *Acts of War: The Behavior of Men in Battle.* New York: The Free Press.

Horowitz, Dan. 1982. "The Israeli Defence Forces: A Civilianized Military in a Partially Militarized Society," in R. Kolkowitz and Y. Karbonski (eds.). *Soldiers, Peasants and Bureaucrats.* London: Allen Lane.

Horowitz, Dan, and Baruch Kimmerling. 1974. "Some Social Implications of Military Service and the Reserves System in Israel." *Archives European de Sociologie* 15: 262–76.

Horowitz, Dan, and Moshe Lissak. 1989. *Trouble in Utopia: The Overburdened Polity of Israel.* Albany: State University of New York Press.

Huntington, Samuel P. 1957. *The Soldier and the State.* Cambridge Mass.: Harvard University Press.

Inbar, Avital. 1989. "Intifada: Only Facts." *Davar* 22 December.

Ingraham, Larry L. 1984. *The Boys in the Barracks.* Philadelphia: ISHI.

Ingraham, Larry L., and Frederick J. Manning. 1981. "Cohesion: Who Needs It, What Is it and How Do We Get It to Them?" *Military Review* 61(6): 2–12.

Janowitz, Morris. 1971. *The Professional Soldier: A Social and Political Portrait.* New York: Free Press.

Kalderon, Nissim. 1988. *The Feeling of Place.* Hakibbutz Hameuchad. (Hebrew)

Kahalani, Avigdor. 1988. *Oz 77.* Jerusalem: Shocken. (Hebrew)

Katriel, Tamar. 1991. *Communal Webs: Communication and Culture in Contemporary Israel.* Albany: State University of New York Press.

Katriel, Tamar, and Pearla Nesher. 1986. "*Gibush:* The Rhetoric of Cohesion in Israeli School Culture." *Comparative Education Review* 30(2): 216–31.

Katz, Pearl. 1990. "Emotional Metaphors, Socialization, and Roles of Drill Sergeants." *Ethos* 18: 457–80.

Keesing, Roger M. 1987. "Models, "Folk" and "Cultural": Paradigms Regained?" In Dorothy Holland and Naomi Quinn (eds.). *Cultural Models in Language and Thought.* Cambridge: Cambridge University Press.

Keegan, John. 1976. *The Face of Battle.* New York: Vintage Books.

Kehoe, Alice B. 1989. "Christianity and War," in Mary LeCron Foster and Robert A. Rubinstein (eds.). *Peace and War: Cross-Cultural Perspectives.* New Brunswick: Transaction.

Kellet, Anthony. 1982. *Combat Motivation: The Behavior of Soldiers in Battle.* Boston: Kluwer.

Kennedy, Mary M. 1979. "Generalizing from Single Case Studies." *Evaluation Quarterly* 3(4): 661–78.

Kennet, Lee. 1987. *G.I. – The American Soldier in World War II.* New York: Scribner's.

Kertzer, David I. 1988. *Ritual, Politics and Power.* New Haven: Yale University Press.

Kimmerling, Baruch. 1984. "Making Conflict a Routine: Cumulative Effects of the Arab-Jewish Conflict Upon Israeli Society," in Moshe Lissak (ed.). *Israeli Society and its Defense Establishment.* London: Frank Cass.

—— 1985. *The Interrupted System.* New Brunswick: Transaction Books.

—— 1993. "Patterns of Militarism in Israel." *European Journal of Sociology* 34: 196–223.

Kleiman, Aharon, and Reuven Pedatzur. 1991. *Rearming Israel: Defense Procurement Through the 1990s.* Boulder: Westview.

Lakoff, George, and Zoltan Kovecses. 1987. "The Cognitive Model of Anger Inherent in American English," in Dorothy Holland and Naomi Quinn (eds.). *Cultural Models in Language and Thought.* Cambridge: Cambridge University Press.

Landau, Uri, and Eliav Zakai. 1994. *In Front of Them and With Them: The Excellence of the Combat Platoon Commander in the IDF.* Tel Aviv: Headquarters of the Chief Educational Officer.

Lang, Kurt. 1972. *Military Institutions and the Sociology of Law.* Beverley Hills: Sage.

Laskov, Hayyim. 1980. "Preface" *The Sharp End of War by John Ellis.* Tel Aviv: Ministry of Defence. (Hebrew)

Lev, Igal. 1984. *First Night Without Mummy.* Tel Aviv: Adar Publishers (Hebrew)

Levin, Marlin, and David Halevy. 1983. "Israel," in Richard A. Gabriel (ed.). *Fighting Armies: Antagonists of the Middle East – A Combat Assessment.* Westport, Conn.: Greenwood.

Levite, Ariel. 1989. *Offense and Defense in Israeli Military Doctrine.* Boulder: Westview.

Levy, Amichai, Eliezer Witztum, Zahava Solomon, Michel Gerank, and Moshe Kotler. 1993. *Combat Reactions in Israel's Wars, 1948–1982.* Tel-Aviv: Medical Corps Command (IDF). (Hebrew)

Liebes, Tamar, and Shoshana Blum-Kulka. 1994. "Managing a Moral Dilemma: Israeli Soldiers in the Intifada." *Armed Forces and Society* 27(1): 45–68.

Lieblich, Amia. 1989. *The Transition to Adulthood During Military Service: The Israeli Case.* Albany: State University of New York Press.

Lieblich, Amia, and Meir Perlow. 1988. "Transition to Adulthood during Military Service." *The Jerusalem Quarterly* 47: 40–76.

Liebman, Charles S., and Eliezer Don-Yehiya. 1983. *Civil Religion in Israel: Traditional Judaism and Political Culture in the Jewish State.* Berkeley: University of California Press.

Linde, Charlotte. 1987. "Explanatory Systems in Oral Life Stories," in Dorothy Holland and Naomi Quinn (eds.). *Cultural Models in Language and Thought.* Cambridge: Cambridge University Press.

Lissak, Moshe. 1984. "Paradoxes of Israeli Civil-Military Relations: An Introduction," in Moshe Lissak (ed.). *Israeli Society and its Defense Establishment.* London: Frank Cass.

Littlewood, Roland. "Military Rape". *Anthropology Today* 13 (2) (1997): 7–16.

Lock, Margaret M. 1993. "Cultivating the Body: Anthropology and Epistemologies of Bodily Practice and Knowledge." *Annual Review of Anthropology* 22: 133–55.

Lofgren, Orvar. 1987. "Deconstructing Swedishness: Culture and Class in Modern Sweden," in Anthony Jackson (ed.). *Anthropology at Home*. London: Tavistock.

Lomsky-Feder, Edna. 1992. "Youth in the Shadow of War – War in the Light of Youth: Life Stories of Israeli Veterans," in Wim Meeus et. al. (eds.). *Adolescence, Careers and Culture*. The Hague: De Gruyter.

—— 1994. "Patterns of Participation in War and the Construction of War in the Life Course: Life Stories of Israeli Veterans From the Yom Kippur War." Ph.D Diss., Hebrew University of Jerusalem.

Lustick, Ian. 1988. *For the Land and the Lord: Jewish Fundamentalism in Israel.* New York: Council on Foreign Relations.

Luttwak, Edward, and Dan Horowitz. 1975. *The Israeli Army*. London: Allen Lane.

Lutz, Catherine A. 1990. "Engendered Emotion: Gender, Power, and the Rhetoric of Emotional Control in American Discourse," in Catherine A. Lutz and Lila Abu-Lughod (eds.). *Language and the Politics of Emotion*. Cambridge: Cambridge University Press.

Mandelbaum, David G. 1989. "Anthropology for the Second Stage of the Nuclear Age," in Mary LeCron Foster and Robert A. Rubinstein (eds.). *Peace and War: Cross-Cultural Perspectives*. New Brunswick: Transaction.

Mann, Michael. 1987. "War and Social Theory: Into Battle with Classes, Nations and States," in Colin Creighton and Martin Shaw, (eds.). *The Sociology of War and Peace*. London: Macmillan.

Marcus George E., and Michael M.J. Fischer. 1986. *Anthropology as Cultural Critique: An Experimental Moment in the Human Sciences*. Chicago: Chicago University Press.

McElhinny, Bonnie. 1994. "An Economy of Affect: Objectivity, Masculinity and the Gendering of Police Work," in Andrea Cornwall and Nancy Lindisfarne (eds.). *Dislocating Masculinity: Comparative Ethnographies*. London: Routledge.

Meiron, Dan. 1987. *If There Is No Jerusalem … Essays on Hebrew Writing in Its Cultural-Political Context*. Tel Aviv: Hakibbutz Hameuchad. (Hebrew)

Melman, Yossi. 1993. *The New Israelis: An Intimate View of a Changing People*. Tel Aviv: Schocken. (Hebrew)

Milgram, Norman A., ed. 1986. *Stress and Coping in Time of War: Generalizations from the Israeli Experience*. New York: Brunner/Mazel Publishers.

Mintz, Alex. 1976. "Military-Industrial Linkages in Israel." *Armed Forces and Society* 12(1): 9–27.

Morgan, David H.J. 1992. *Discovering Men*. London: Routledge.

—— 1994. "Theater of War: Combat, the Military and Masculinities," in Harry Brod and Michael Kaufman (eds.). *Theorizing Masculinities*. Thousand Oaks: Sage.

Morgan, Gareth. 1986. *Images of Organization*. Beverly Hills: Sage.

Moskos, Charles C. 1975. "The American Combat Soldier in Vietnam." *Journal of Social Issues* 31(4): 25–37.

—— 1988. *Soldiers and Sociology*. Washington D.C.: U.S. Government Printing Office.

Mosse, George L. 1990. *Fallen Soldiers: Reshaping the Memory of the World Wars*. Oxford: Oxford University Press.

Ofrat, Gideon. 1991. "The Fading of the Khaki: The Image of the Soldier in Israeli Art." *Studio* 27: 6–12. (Hebrew)

—— 1994. "How Have Heros Fallen: Israeli Art Fights Heros." *Mishkafaim* 22: 39–45. (Hebrew)

Ortner, Sherry B. 1973. "On Key Symbols." *American Anthropologist* 75: 1338–46.

Ortony, A. 1975. "Why metaphors are necessary and not just nice." *Educational Theory* 25(1): 456–53.

Orum, Anthony M., Joe R. Feagin, and Gideon Sjoberg. 1991. "Introduction: The Nature of the Case Study," in Joe R. Feagin, Anthony Orum and Gideon Sjoberg (eds.). *A Case for the Case Study*. Chapel Hill: University of North Carolina Press.

Paine, Robert. 1992 "Anthropology Beyond the Routine: Cultural Alternatives for the Handling of the Unexpected," *international Journal of Moral and Social Studies* 7(3): 183–203.

Peacock, James L. 1986. *The Anthropological Lens: Harsh Light, Soft Focus*. Cambridge: Cambridge University Press.

Pelto, Peritti J., and Gretel H. 1970. *Anthropological Research: The Structure of Inquiry*. Cambridge: Cambridge University Press.

Peri, Yoram. 1981. "Political-Military Partnership in Israel," *international Political Science Review* 2(3): 303–15.

—— 1993. "The Arab-Israeli Conflict and Israeli Democracy," in Ehud Sprinzak and Larry Diamond (eds.). *Israeli Democracy Under Stress*. Boulder: Lynne Rienner.

Quinn, Naomi. 1987. "Convergent Evidence for a Cultural Model of American Marriage," in Dorothy Holland and Naomi Quinn (eds.). *Cultural Models in Language and Thought*. Cambridge: Cambridge University Press.

Quinn, Naomi, and Dorothy Holland. 1987. "Culture and Cognition," in Dorothy Holland and Naomi Quinn (eds.). *Cultural Models in Language and Thought*. Cambridge: Cambridge University Press.

Richardson, F.M. 1978. *Fighting Spirit: A Study of Psychological Factors in War*. London: Leo Cooper.

Rieber, Robert W., and Robert J. Kelly. 1991. "Substance and Shadow: Images of the Enemy," in Robert W. Rieber (ed.). *The Psychology of War and Peace: The Image of the Enemy*. New York: Plenum.

Ronen, Avihu. 1993. "Four Traditions of Leadership in the IDF," in Micha Poper and Avihu Ronen (eds.). *On Leadership*. Tel Aviv: Ministry of Defence. (Hebrew)

Rosaldo, Michelle. 1980. *Knowledge and Passion: Ilongot Notions of Self and Social Life*. Cambridge: Cambridge University Press.

Rosenthal, Ruvik. 1989. *The Family of the Beaufort*. Tel Aviv: Ha'Poalim. (Hebrew)

Rothberg, Gunther E. 1979. *The Anatomy of the Israeli Army*. London: B.T. Batsford Ltd.

Rubin, Nissan. 1985. "Unofficial Memorial Rites in an Army Unit." *Social Forces* 63(3): 795–809.

Schiff, Rebecca L. 1995. "Civil-Military Relations Reconsidered: A Theory of Concordance." *Armed Forces and Society* 22(1): 7–24.

Schiff, Ze'ev, and Ehud Ya'ari. 1990. *Intifada*. Jerusalem: Schocken. (Hebrew)

Schild, E.O. 1973. "On the Meaning of Military Service in Israel," in Michael Curtis and Mordecai S. Chertoff (eds.). *Israel: Social Structure and Change*. New Brunswick: Transaction.

Schon, Donald A. 1987. "The Art of Managing: Reflection-in-Action within and Organizational Learning System," in Paul Rabinow and William Sullivan (eds.). *Interpretive Social Science: A Second Look*. Berkeley: University of California Press.

Schwartz, Barry, Yael Zerubavel, and Bernice M. Barnett. 1986. "The Recovery of Masada: A Study in Collective Memory." *The Sociological Quarterly* 27(2): 147–64.

Segal, David R., and H. Wallace Sinaiko, eds. 1986. *Life in the Rank and File*. Washington D.C.: Pergamon-Brassey's.

Shafritz, Jay M., Todd J. A. Shafritz, and David Robertson. 1989. *The Facts on File Dictionary of Military Science*. New York: Facts on File.

Shalit, Ben. 1988. *The Psychology of Conflict and Combat*. New York: Praeger.

Shatan, Chaim F. 1977. "Bogus Manhood, Bogus Honor: Surrender and Transfiguration in the United States Marine Corps." *Psychoanalytic Review* 64: 586–610.

Shaw, Martin. 1988. *Dialectics of War: An Essay in the Social Theory of Total War and Peace*. London: Pluto Press.

Shaw, Martin, and Colin Creighton. 1987. "Introduction," in Colin Creighton and Martin Shaw (eds.). *The Sociology of War and Peace*. London: Macmillan.

Shay, Jonathan. 1995. *Achilles in Vietnam: Combat Trauma and the Undoing of Character*. New York: Touchstone.

Sheffy, Yigal. 1991. *Officer's Badge: Training and Education of the Haganah Officers*. Tel Aviv: Ministry of Defence Press.

Shirom, Arie. 1976. On Some Correlates of Combat Performance. *Administrative Science Quarterly* 21: 419–32.

Simons, Anna. 1997. *The Company They Keep: Life Inside the U.S. Army Special Forces*. New York: Free Press.

Sion, Liora. 1997. "Images of Manhood among Combat Soldiers: Military Service in Israel's Infantry Brigades as a Rite of Passage from Youthhood to Adulthood." Masters thesis, The Hebrew University of Jerusalem.

Sivan, Emmanuel. 1991. *The 1948 Generation: Myth, Profile and Memory.* Tel Aviv: Ministry of Defense. (Hebrew)

Sjoberg, Gideon, Norma Williams, Ted Vaughan, and Andree F. Sjoberg. 1991. "The Case Study Approach in Social Research: Basic Methodological Issues," in Joe R. Feagin, Anthony M. Orum, and Gideon Sjoberg (eds.). *A Case for the Case Study.* Chapel Hill: University of North Carolina Press.

Solomon, Zahava, Karni Ginzburg, Yuval Neria, and Abraham Ohry. 1995. "Coping with War Captivity: The Role of Sensation Seeking." *European Journal of Personality* 9: 57–70.

Tilly, Charles, ed. 1985. *The Formation of National States in Western Europe.* Princeton: Princeton University Press.

Van Creveld, Martin. 1977. "Military Lessons of the Yom-Kippur War." *The Jerusalem Quarterly* 5:114–24.

—— 1985. *Command in War.* Cambridge, Mass.: Harvard University Press.

—— 1983. *Fighting Power: German and US Army Performance, 1939–1945.* London: Arms and Armour Press.

Van Gelder, Malcolm, and Michael J. Eley. 1986. "Anzacs, Chockos, and Diggers: A Portrait of the Australian Enlisted Man," in David R. Segal and H. Wallace Sinaiko (eds.). *Life in the Rank and File: Enlisted Men and Women in the Armed Forces of the United States, Australia, Canada, and the United Kingdom.* Washington, D.C.: Pergamon-Brassey's.

Van Maanen, John, and Gideon Kunda. 1989. "'Real Feelings': Emotional Expression and Organizational Culture." *Research in Organizational Behavior* 11: 43–103.

Veiler, Yosef. 1991. "Between Hero and Whore." *Politika* 39: 57–61. (Hebrew)

Wald, Emanuel. 1992. *The Wald Report: The Decline of Israeli National Security Since 1967.* Boulder: Westview.

Walker, Wallace Earl. 1992. "Comparing Army Reserve Forces: A Tale of Multiple Ironies, Conflicting Realities, and More Certain Prospects." *Armed Forces and Society* 18(3): 303–22.

Weisburd, David, and Vered Vinitzky. 1984. "Vigilantism as Rational Control: The Case of Gush Emunim Settlers," in Myron J. Aronoff (ed.). *Cross-Currents in Israeli Culture and Politics.* New Brunswick: Transaction.

Williams, Louis. 1989. *Israel Defense Forces: A People's Army.* Tel Aviv: Ministry of Defense Publishing House.

Yin, Robert K. 1981. "The Case Study Crisis: Some Answers." *Administrative Science Quarterly* 26: 58–65.

Yuval-Davis, Nira. 1987. "Front and Rear: The Sexual Division of Labour in the Israeli Army," in Haleh Afshar (ed.). *Women, State and Ideology: Studies from Africa and Asia.* London: Macmillan.

INDEX